WHAT IS AISH?

AN OVERVIEW OF AISH'S PHILOSOPHY
AND MISSION AS EXPRESSED IN THE
TEACHINGS OF **RABBI NOAH WEINBERG**

Compiled and Edited by Tzvi Gluckin

ISBN: 978-0-9845856-5-6

Aish
Dan Family Aish World Center
One Western Wall Plaza
Old City, Jerusalem

US Headquarters:
915 Clifton Avenue, Suite #4
Clifton, NJ 07013

www.aish.com

You can reach the author at tgluckin@aish.com

Prepared for press by Estie@EDPressSolutions.com
Cover design by REM90, www.REM90.com

This project would not have been possible without the audio files, research materials, outlines, and other resources available at Aish United (Aish's internal intranet site), particularly Rabbi Eric Coopersmith's transcriptions of Rabbi Weinberg's classes, together with Rabbi Zev Pomeranz's sources and notes. Rabbi Daniel Schloss' vast library of original documents was an invaluable resource as well. Special thanks to Rabbis Steven Burg and Elliot Mathias for helping to conceive of and supporting this project.

Printed in the United States of America

10 9 8 7 6 5 4 3 2

Contents

Forward

By Rabbi Steven Burg,
CEO Aish Global

According to the Talmud, a great sage once claimed that if Jewish wisdom were to disappear, he would restore it with his keen analytical skills and towering intellect. His colleague countered that the better way would be to gather eleven students, teach five of them one book each from the Five Books of Moses, teach the other six one order each from the Six Orders of the Mishna—the primary work of the Oral Law—and then instruct them to teach each other.

A great leader, despite his brilliance, charisma, and natural gifts, cannot alone solve the problems that face the Jewish people. Rather, everyone, young and old alike, even children— even you—have a role to play. Too many Jews have lost touch with their heritage and raison d'être. Too many Jews don't know what it means to be a Jew. This is the heart and soul of what Aish is all about.

Aish is a movement rooted in the idea that if you know something, you have an obligation to teach it. If Jewish wisdom—even something basic, even a simple idea—has impacted you or made a difference in your life, you need to share that wisdom with someone else.

This was the philosophy of the founder and charismatic leader of Aish, Rabbi Noah Weinberg, of blessed memory. He understood that when you hear something, and it makes sense to you, you must tell it over. If you discover something like the secret of happiness, or the definition of love, or the tools to infuse your life with purpose and meaning—which comprise some of Rabbi Weinberg's core teachings—how can you possibly keep that a secret? In effect, our job is to share the love.

In truth, it's so much more than that. Aish wasn't founded simply to share Jewish ideas, as amazing as those may be. Aish is a movement—with a focus on the soul of the Jewish people—to transform the tenor and feel of what it means to be a Jew. Jewish identity must be rooted in something more than remembering the Holocaust, or eating bagels, or sharing a unique sense of humor. A Jewish identity, rooted in authentic Jewish wisdom, will have depth, and—when we reach a critical mass of Jews alive today—will have the power to change the world for the good.

According to our current Rosh Yeshiva, Rabbi Yitzchak Berkovits, to return to what it means to be a Jew, every Jew needs to know, or at least be aware of, three things:

- that God exists;
- that God gave the Torah to the Jewish people;
- and, that the Torah is meaningful and relevant to your life.

Rabbi Gluckin has done a masterful job in creating a tome that encapsulates Aish's philosophy and operating principles to ensure that every Jew comes to know these three tenets of our faith. This book reflects the heart of our movement, and what we believe.

I know you will enjoy reading about the novel approach of Aish. Welcome to the family!

"At least we know we're crazy."

Introduction

When Rabbi Noah Weinberg passed away in 2009, he left behind a vast body of teachings that form the core philosophy of Aish HaTorah, the organization he founded in 1974. That material exists as hundreds of audio recordings (some of which have been transcribed), as well as numerous books, anthologies, and articles on aish.com. Many of his students have also written books, and created programs, based on his teachings.

However, despite that, none of that content exists in one place. There's no single book or work you can point to that clearly sums up Rabbi Weinberg's philosophy or Aish's educational mission. No place that says, "This is what Aish is about. This is what Aish is telling the world."

That's the point of this little book. It attempts to compile—from the vast corpus of Rabbi Weinberg's thought—a clear, concise, overview of what Aish believes, and the core ideas that define the movement.

The aim here is to be thorough, while also keeping it short. Many of the sections you're about to read were taken from hour-long classes, and can easily be expanded. Together with sources, this could become a 500-page dissertation, and indeed, someone is already working on that. But that's not what this project is about.

Rabbi Weinberg's overall philosophy falls into two general categories: God and responsibility, and that's how this content is organized as well.

"God" includes not just the Jewish definition of God—which, as the basis of ethical monotheism, changed the world—but also your responsibility to know that God exists; to know that God created the world for your benefit and pleasure; and to see God's hand in your life.

God is the point of many of Rabbi Weinberg's most popular teachings: the highest level of pleasure is a relationship with God, the highest level of free will is "to make your will His will," the highest level of prayer is to listen to God's messages, and the highest level of love is for true friends to know that "God is their third friend." It's also the secret of happiness, the point of being an intellectual, the message of the ABCs of Judaism, and on and on.

As you'll see as you read on, you can't understand, or explain, Aish's message without including God.

"Responsibility" refers to both your personal responsibility—meaning that you are responsible for your happiness and success—as well as feeling personally responsible for the Jewish people's national mission.

In 2006, on a trip to Poland that visited the Nazi death camps, as well as the former, once vibrant, Polish Jewish communities—which included abandoned and desecrated yeshivas, synagogues, and homes—Rabbi Weinberg expressed his outrage, "Look at these *farshtunken* Nazis," he said (I am paraphrasing, although I am not paraphrasing the word *farshtunken*, that's a quote). "Look at what they accomplished. They worked together. They innovated. They improved their methods. They learned from each other ... and they managed to kill six million of us. Imagine what we could accomplish if we would work together and learn from each other."

You can change the world. As a part of the Jewish people, you're a member of the greatest team ever assembled, surrounded by the world's most innovative and original thinkers. Learn from them, share what you know, and don't lose sight of your Father in heaven, who—if you allow Him to help you—will give you everything you need to succeed.

*"The battle for life
is the battle for sanity."*

Part I:
God

Section One:
Rational Belief

God Created The World For You

God's existence is central to Jewish belief, and central to how you are supposed to live your life. According to Jewish thought, God is the omnipotent, infinite, all-powerful source of existence. He created the world, sustains it, and oversees everything that happens throughout the totality of existence.[1]

Take that idea to its logical extreme: God is the *only* power. Everything that happens—anywhere and at all times— only does so because of His direct, intimate, and constant involvement. Even something as minute as maintaining the relationship between an electron and an atom's nucleus—and that goes for every atom everywhere in the universe—only happens as a result of God's direct, intimate, and constant involvement.

Nothing exists or happens independent of God's will.

And that's a good thing, because God created you, too. He is intimately involved in your life. He is the only power—the

---

1. Maimonides, Hilchos Yesodei Hatorah, 1:1: "All of existence—the heavens, earth, and everything in between—only exists because of the truth of [God's] being." See the whole chapter.

only reality—and He created everything, as in all of existence, for you.[2]

You're Commanded To Know That

The Torah, in Deuteronomy 4:39, commands you to know that God exists. "Know it today and ponder it in your heart: God is the Supreme Being in heaven above and on the earth below. There is no other."

Yet that statement contains a logical discrepancy: if you know God exists, and that He—as the author of the Torah—is the one commanding you, then it's unnecessary to know that He exists. You know that already. And if you don't believe in God, why would you listen to a commandment that's written in the Torah?

The point is that the Torah is telling you to be an independent, critical thinker. That's a commandment. Belief in God isn't something you should just accept, even if that's what your society, parents, and teachers believe. You need to gather evidence, work through the details, and come to an understanding on your own.

That's your obligation as a Jew: to know.

Knowledge is the highest level. It's a conviction—or an intuitive perception—based on an overabundance of evidence.

For example, you know you have five fingers. You don't need to be convinced that you have five fingers. You just need to look at your hand. The evidence is overwhelming. If someone brought evidence that you had a different number of fingers, that evidence wouldn't shake your confidence. You're clear. That's the level of clarity you're expected to attain about your beliefs and values as well.

---

2. Really, God created the world for your benefit and pleasure (see below). *Path of the Just*, chapter 1

BELIEF

But knowledge is just one level of awareness, another level—although it's considered a weaker conviction than knowledge[3]—is belief.

Belief is based on evidence. The amount, or quality, of the evidence may not be complete or foolproof, but it's enough to make a decision. For example, a court of law will decide against a person—which may result in him losing his life, his children, his money, his business, or going to jail—based on the evidence, even though the judge and jury will never know with the same level of certainty as the witnesses.

Belief is considered the starting point.[4] You should not take a leap of faith. You need at least enough evidence to say that you're making an intelligent, informed decision. You may not even have total clarity, but you have integrity, and your decision is the best possibility based on the information available. Your job is to then gather more evidence until, ultimately, you can say your convictions are based on knowledge.

BLIND FAITH

Belief and knowledge are convictions based on evidence. Faith is not. Faith—as in blind faith—is a leap against logic. In Jewish thought, blind faith is called "bad belief."[5] It's a product of desire, or something you *want* to be true, even though you're lacking evidence. It's also anathema to how a Jew is supposed

---

3. Psalm 92:3: "להגיד בבקר חסדך ואמונתך בלילות"

4. *The Way of God*, Chapter 1: "Every Jew must *believe* and *know* that there is a first cause …" Belief is the starting point. Knowledge is the goal. (Heard from Rav Yitzchak Berkovits)

5. Rabbi Weinberg translated *emunah tefailah* as "bad belief," and based on what I can find, that seems to be original to him. The closest thing to a source is Job 13:4, "But you are all inventors of lies" (ואולם אתם טפלי שקר).

to think, which is predicated on rational belief, and starts with gathering evidence and asking questions.

Society

Similar to taking a leap of faith are the ideas you accept uncritically, which are those you absorb from your society. These ideas aren't necessarily bad or even wrong, it's just that you've accepted them without thinking. They're the axioms you take for granted, or that you heard from your parents, teachers, friends, or peers; or that you picked up from the media and popular culture. They are powerful and persuasive.

But are they true?

You need independence to acquire wisdom. Your parents have an obligation to teach you a philosophy of life—and hopefully they encouraged you to ask questions and to think about your answers—but you have an obligation to *make that your own*. You have to make sure it is true, which requires independent thinking. Without that, you're just accepting what you've heard.

How do you know you're right?

Every Person Has The Ability To Recognize Truth

Deep in the belly of your consciousness lies the knowledge you need to live a purposeful and meaningful life. The information is already there. You need to access it.

In Rabbi Weinberg's class, "Know What You Know," he distinguishes between *yediyah* (knowledge), *emunah* (belief), and *emunah tefailah* (bad belief, or faith).

According to the Talmud,[6] before you were born—while you were still a fetus in your mother's womb—an angel[7] taught you Jewish wisdom. You absorbed everything it taught you. But moments before birth, it touched you under your nose—making an indentation (called the philtrum)—and you forgot what you learned.

That story teaches a powerful truth: you were born equipped with wisdom. Your soul already knows everything there is to know about life—it was programmed in the womb—you just need to remember. As you make your way through life, and you're exposed to different ideas, certain ideas will resonate. It's as if you've heard them before.

That's because you have.

---

6. The story is adapted from Niddah 30B: "A candle is lit for [the fetus in the womb] above its head, and it gazes from one end of the world to the other, like it says (Job 29:3), 'When His lamp shined above my head, and by His light I walked through darkness.' ... And [the fetus] is taught the entire Torah, as it says (Proverbs 4:4), 'And He taught me and said to me, let your heart hold fast my words. Keep my commandments, and live.' ... But once [the fetus] emerges into the airspace of the world, an angel comes and slaps it on its mouth, causing it to forget the entire Torah, as it says (Genesis 4:7), 'Sin crouches at the door.' ... [The fetus also] doesn't leave the womb until it swears an oath ... 'Be righteous and do not be wicked. And even if the whole world tells you that you are righteous, consider yourself wicked. And know that the Holy One, Blessed be He, is pure, and His ministers are pure, and that the soul that He gave you is pure. If you keep [your soul] pure, good, and if not, I will take it from you.'" Also see the *Midrash Tanchuma, Pekudei* 3, for a more elaborate version of this story.

7. The Hebrew word for angel is "*malach* (מלאך)," which means "messenger." It can also mean "work." In other words, an angel is a "messenger" from God that carries out His "work." It's a metaphysical concept that helps explain how God's will becomes manifest in the mundane, physical world. In a similar vein, the English word "angel" comes from the Greek word "angelos," which means "messenger" or "agent." (Adapted from: https://aish.com/angels/)

Every person is born with the ability to recognize truth, and you don't need to travel the world looking for it. It's right under your nose.

Being Jewish isn't an accident of birth. God runs the world, and He made you Jewish on purpose. Jewish wisdom is your heritage. Don't reject it out of hand. Check it out. Chances are, you're already familiar with it.

GOD CREATED THE WORLD FOR YOUR BENEFIT AND PLEASURE

God created the world for your benefit and pleasure. In prayer, God is called, "Our Father, Our King," and "Our Father, the Merciful."[8] According to the Talmud,[9] God, similar to many parents, is happy when you're happy, and feels your pain when you're suffering. He created the world for you, and He wants you to enjoy it.

That idea is implicit in the Torah as well. In the book of Genesis, when God first created people, He placed them in the Garden of Eden. "Eden" is the Hebrew word for "pleasure." Man was created for pleasure, and put in a situation where he could earn the maximum pleasure.

---

8. In the daily liturgy, in the second blessing before the Shema, God is called both "Our Father, Our King (אבינו מלכנו)," as well as, "Our Father, the Merciful (אבינו האב הרחמן)." "Our Father, Our King" is also the theme of a communal prayer recited on the High Holidays and public fast days. Also see Exodus 4:22: "You must say to Pharaoh, 'Israel is my son, my first born.'"

9. *Taanis* 16A: "Why [in Talmudic times, as part of a public fast that was declared due to lack of rain] do we place ashes on the ark? Rabbi Yehudah ben Pazi says, it's as if to say (Psalms 91:15), 'I [God] am with him in his distress.' Reish Lakish says (Isaiah 63:9), 'In their every distress, He [God] is in distress.' Rabbi Zeira says, 'At first, when I saw the rabbis placing ashes on the ark, my entire body trembled.'"

But that raises a number of questions, which, when answered, helps explain how you're supposed to look at your life.

One: If God created the world for your benefit and pleasure, then why does it look like it does? The world is a mess. Couldn't God do a better job?

Answer: No. Ultimately, the true, infinite pleasure God is offering transcends this finite, limited world.

Two: But if that's the case, why not just create paradise, and forego the struggles of this world?

Answer: This world is temporary. It's the place to work and prepare—to become the person you're capable of becoming—to labor and toil.

Three: But why make man work? Why not just place him in a situation where he doesn't need to work and prepare? Why not give him infinite, transcendent pleasure as a gift?

Answer: Receiving a gift is like getting something for nothing (in the Talmud, that's called, "bread of shame"). Receiving a handout makes you feel awkward and uncomfortable. True, authentic pleasure is something you earn independently, by yourself.[10]

Four: But couldn't God create a world where you don't have to work? Where you can receive a gift *without* experiencing shame?

Answer: No. And that's because the greatest pleasure—and the whole point of existence—is to be like God. God

---

10. *Daas Tevunos*, Rabbi Moshe Chaim Luzzatto (page 5 of the Friedlander edition): "In order to bestow the best possible good, God knew that it was appropriate that the recipient [man] should receive [his reward] as a result of his own efforts. [Man] would then *own* that good, and would not be left with any shame for having received [a handout]. Like it says in the Jerusalem Talmud (*Orla* 1:3), 'One who eats that which isn't his, is embarrassed to look at [his benefactor] in the face' (נהמא דכיסופא)." (paraphrased from the original)

doesn't receive gifts. He creates. If you're like God, you do that as well. Life, despite the hardships—or maybe because of the hardships—is the opportunity to create yourself, and to actualize your potential.

In other words, the greatest gift—and your ultimate pleasure—is the opportunity to emulate, and, as a consequence of that, have a relationship with God.

GRATITUDE

That awareness—that God gave you the opportunity and independence to emulate Him—comes at a cost, and that cost is gratitude. You have to learn to appreciate the good that God does for you—to give up the illusion that you alone are responsible for your achievements—and to admit that everything you accomplish is because of the opportunities, or gifts, given to you by God.

THE TORAH IS YOUR INSTRUCTIONS FOR LIFE

Jewish practice isn't built around empty, meaningless rituals. It's a set of tools that enables you to live a productive and meaningful life, which means maximizing your pleasure and emulating God. Those tools are found in the Torah.

The word "Torah" means "instructions." The Torah is called "Torat Chaim (תורת חיים)," which means "Instructions for Living." Most simple appliances come with instructions, as do more complex systems and tasks. Life, which is even more complicated, comes with instructions as well, and God, mankind's creator, gave the Torah—or His instructions—to the Jewish people.

The Torah is not a guarantee. It's a system, and its rote, perfunctory application is not enough. It requires consistent, regular study; constant awareness; and a willingness to change, experiment, introspect, innovate, and grow. It's a tool to bring

God into your world, and will teach you to see His hand in your life.

But it can be difficult, too, and you will sometimes fail. But that's ok. You're not expected to be perfect. You're expected to do the work.[11]

SIN VS. MISTAKE

Those failings are called "mistakes," not "sins." The Western notion of sin—an immoral act or rebellion against God—is not the Jewish notion of sin. The Hebrew word, *chet* (חטא), which is usually translated as "sin," actually means "to miss." It's as if you're aiming an arrow, but miss the target,[12] or in other words, a "mistake." Mistakes are solvable problems—you can grow and move on—sins are not.

The Hebrew language does have other words that denote more serious moral failings, like *avon* (עוון), usually translated as "iniquity," but meaning a rationalization or faulty reasoning; *pesha* (פשע), referring to someone who denies the Torah's validity; and *avaira* (עבירה), which is crossing a line, or a transgression.[13]

According to the Talmud, you only err when overcome by an "insane spirit (רוח שטות),[14]" which explains why some Biblical expressions of "sin" are associated with "confusion."[15] Con-

---

11. *Avos* 2:20: "Rabbi Tarfon says, 'The day is short, the task is abundant, the laborers are lazy, the wage is great, and the master of the house is insistent.'" *Avos* 2:21: "He used to say, 'You are not required to complete the task, yet you are [also] not free to withdraw from it.'"

12. In the Bible, the word "*chet*" means "to miss." See Judges 20:16: "Among these people were 700 of the best left-handed men. Every one of them could sling a stone at a hair and not miss (ולא יחטא)."

13. These translations are from the Artscroll *Viduy Yom Kippur Companion*

14. *Sotah* 3A: "A person does not commit a transgression unless a spirit of foolishness enters him."

15. For example, see Psalms 38:6. According to the *Metzudas Dovid*, "אולתי," which is "folly," means being possessed by an "insane spirit" (see note

fusion and ignorance are considered dangerous and contagious diseases. Unlike other belief systems, the Torah teaches that man is born with an inherent desire to do good, but ignorance perverts and corrupts that desire. The antidote to being ignorant is studying the Torah, the life instructions God gave to the Jewish people.[16]

---

above)

16. *Kiddushin* 30B: "God says, 'I created the evil inclination (יצר הרע), and I created the Torah as its antidote. If you study the Torah, you won't be handed over to the evil inclination ... If you encounter the disgusting one (the evil inclination) along the road, pull him into the study hall."

Section Two:
Living With God

You're commanded to know that God exists. But gathering evidence, and coming to an intellectual understanding of God's existence is not enough. You also need to internalize that idea, and make it your own.

Knowing something isn't the same as believing it.

According to the Talmud, over time, the Torah's overall approach to life was distilled into just one general idea, "Habakkuk came and established [all the Torah's commandments] upon one [principle], (based on Habakkuk 2:4): 'The righteous person lives with his belief.'"[17]

In other words, *the* foundational principle of being a Jew—the point of the Torah and its commandments—is to instill within you an awareness of the reality of God's existence. Many people think they believe in God, but the Talmud's

---

17. *Makkot* 24A: "David came and established the [Torah's 613 commandments] on 11 ... Isaiah came and established them on six ... Micah came and established them on three ... Isaiah then came and established them on two ... and then Habakkuk came and established [all the Torah's commandments] upon one [principle], (based on Habakkuk 2:4): 'The righteous person lives with his belief.'" See the Talmud for a complete list of the different commandments considered to encompass "all 613 commandments."

message is that that's not an easy idea to grasp: it takes a lifetime of effort, and is the goal of living a Jewish life.

The Torah's tool to keep that awareness of God at the forefront of your consciousness is six commandments—or mitzvahs—that you're supposed to do *constantly*. A "constant" mitzvah is a goal—it's a state of being—and it's a necessity because people, by nature, are constantly distracted.

The Six Constant Mitzvahs

1. Know God exists
2. Don't believe in other powers
3. Know God is one
4. Love God
5. Fear God
6. Don't stray after your heart and mind

Know God Exists

As mentioned earlier, the Torah, in Deuteronomy 4:39, commands you to "Know it today and *ponder it in your heart*: God is the Supreme Being in heaven above and on the earth below. There is no other."

In addition to an intellectual relationship with God, you also need an emotional connection. In prayer, also as mentioned above, God is referred to as your "Father in Heaven." He created the world for your benefit and pleasure.

God is compared to a parent to teach you that just like your parents love you, God loves you as well. He loves you with that same type of unconditional love.

That's a hard idea to wrap your head around, yet internalizing it—or wrestling with it, or coming to grips with it—is central to understanding your purpose and meaning in life. God can do anything, and yet He decided to create you. That means you are central to creation. You're here for a reason. He made you on purpose, and your life—and the things that happen to you—have purpose and meaning as well.

Living with that idea is called trust, or *bitachon* (בטחון), and with daily reflection and introspection, is something you can acquire. In Jewish thought, part of that work includes meditating on seven ideas:[18]

One: Realize that God loves you.

As alien as that idea may seem, you probably already believe it. It's at least something you're intuitively in touch with. If you've ever turned to prayer in times of trouble or need, ask yourself, where does that come from? Calling out to God—usually in desperation—is something intrinsic to the human condition, and it stems from an intuitive, internal understanding that God exists, that He loves you, and that He's someone to turn to when circumstances hit the proverbial fan.

Getting in touch with that intuitive part of your psyche—a side of yourself you probably take for granted, or don't think about very often—can be uncomfortable. Yet it's part of your programming. How did it get there?

Two: Realize that God's awareness is constant.

God, by definition, is infinite. He's aware of everything that happens in the totality of the cosmos. He hears your requests—He knows what you want—and that's something you may intuitively feel, too. That may also explain why so many people, in study after study,[19] claim not only that God hears their prayers, but answers them as well.

---

18. *Duties of the Heart*, Gate of Trust, Chapter 3

19. Rabbi Weinberg often quoted a study from *Time Magazine* (that was decades old). This is from *Vox*, although the percentage of people who say God answers their prayers is qualified with "amongst people who pray." https://www.vox.com/2014/10/6/6918427/lots-of-americans-pray-heres-what-they-pray-for-study

Three: Realize that God has all the power.

God is the source of reality. The world is His, and He can do, literally, anything. He has the ability to give you anything you desire.

Four: Realize that God is the *only* power.

Nothing happens that God doesn't allow to happen. God sustains the universe—every creature, every blade of grass[20]— every second. No creation is sustained without Him. Nothing can stop Him, and no one can help Him.[21] He is all there is.

Five: Realize that since God is the only power, everything He does for you is a gift.

Whatever you request from God is nothing compared to what He's already given you. For example, consider the fact that you're able to see. Even if you ask God for an insane amount of money, that's nothing compared to the eyes He gave you for free. That applies to everything: your other five senses; that you can think, have what to eat, have people who love you; that you can feel the warmth of the sun, and so much more. Appreciating that everything is a gift—and that God constantly helps you—teaches you to trust Him. You can depend on Him, and He will continue giving you everything you need.

Six: God doesn't need anything from you.

Whether or not you keep the Torah doesn't affect God. It affects you. God gave the Torah to you for your benefit. Think of it as an opportunity. If you choose to follow its rules, it will enhance your life. If you don't, it won't. But regardless, it's an opportunity for *you*. Not for God.

Seven: God knows what's good for you.

---

20. *Bereshit Rabbah* 10:6: "Every blade of grass has a spiritual force (מזל) that strikes it, and tells it, 'Grow.'"

21. Isaiah 44:6: "I am first and I am last, and there is no god besides me."

Trusting God means understanding that even when He *doesn't* give you something, He's sending you a message. He's trying to wake you up, to reconnect you to reality.

God may not always give you what you want, but everything He does—including not giving you everything your heart desires—is for your benefit.

Internalizing these seven points is how you come to know—not just intellectually, but emotionally as well—and to live with the reality that God exists, which is the primary purpose of living a Jewish life.

DON'T BELIEVE IN OTHER POWERS

In Jewish thought, a negative commandment—like "don't kill," or "don't eat ham"—only applies when you're tempted to transgress it. If you're not apoplectic with rage at a wrong done to you, or locked in a kitchen overflowing with bacon, then, for the most part, the negative commandment doesn't apply.

Yet the prohibition against believing in other powers is considered a "constant" commandment, which implies that the desire to believe in other powers is a constant temptation.

According to the Talmud,[22] the Biblical verse, "There shall be no strange god *within* you," refers to the strange god that lives *within* a person. That's the ego, or "evil inclination (יצר הרע)," and it's *always* whispering in your ear. It never stops. Your ego—that "other" power—is constantly distracting you from reality. It attempts to take God out of the picture, and obfuscate the fact that so much of what you have—including your intelligence and natural talents—are in reality, gifts from God.

---

22. *Shabbos* 105B: "What is the [meaning of the] verse (Psalms 81:10), 'There shall be no strange god *within* you, nor should you bow before an alien god?' What is the strange god that [lives] *inside* a person? You have to say it's the evil inclination."

And it does that *constantly*.

God is the source of everything, and—if you're clear, and willing to work—He can give you even more. But you have to believe that. Feeling inadequate, defeated, or just saying "I can't," is, in effect, like believing in other powers (as in your ego, or the voice of your evil inclination). The Jewish approach is you most definitely can. God is with you. You cannot fail.

Know God Is One

The highest level of wisdom is comprehending God's oneness. More than knowing that God exists, and greater than not believing in other powers, is understanding that God's existence is the only existence. *Nothing* exists other than God.

As mentioned above: that's the point of Judaism, so much so that you're commanded to meditate on that idea at least twice a day.[23]

Without going too far down a philosophical rabbit hole, God doesn't change. Relative to God (or from God's perspective), creating the world changed nothing.[24] God is who He is. What *did* change is the concept of "perspective." The creation of the world is, in reality, simply the ability of the world's inhabitants (i.e. you), to perceive themselves as separate, or independent, from God.[25]

---

23. You're commanded to say—and to meditate on, and to contemplate—the Shema (Deuteronomy 6:4) every morning and evening. "Listen, Israel. God is our Lord. God is one."

24. Appreciate the impossibility of this idea: you can't even ask the question, "What came before God created the world?" because "before" implies time, and in the beginning, God created time. An idea like "before" is a function of time, and "before" can't exist if time doesn't exist. You can't have something "before" time. That's impossible. And that should give you a headache.

25. "It is this very dual perspective of a single reality that is unchanged before

That's not an illusion. That's real. You're real. You perceive yourself as independent, have the free will to choose, and the ability to act upon those choices. But that's only from your perspective. From God's perspective, nothing's changed.[26]

God did that in order to enable man to earn eternal pleasure; and the ultimate, eternal, only true pleasure is attachment to God.[27] God is all there is. However, God gave a semblance of autonomy to man. You have a mind of your own, and that gives you the opportunity to discover your true source (God), and receive pleasure from your awareness of God's presence. The challenge of being a physical human being is seeing past that perception of autonomy, and discerning the truth of God's existence.

That also explains the existence of evil. Since your purpose in life is to earn eternal pleasure, overcoming challenges is how you attain it. In sports, a great coach makes your life difficult. He understands your weaknesses, and focuses on them, and pushes you, in order to make you great. It's hard. It hurts.

---

and after the creation process that allows us to understand how the creation process is, and is also described by R. Chaim [Volozhin] as being, both concealment and simultaneously also of revelation … The creation process simply *conceals* [God's] existence and thereby *reveals* the existence of this world as a seemingly separate entity in its own right from our perspective, separated from the context of God's existence. This is to the extent that R. Chaim states that we are 'able to imagine, with eyes of flesh, that this world has a reality and existence of its own.'" *Nefesh HaTzimtzum Volume 2*, by Avinoam Fraenkel, page 101. See the full quote and continuation for a deeper understanding of this idea.

26. Exodus 33:20: "A man cannot see me and live."

27. *Path of the Just*, Chapter 1, Rabbi Moshe Chaim Luzzatto: "Man was created for the sole purpose of rejoicing in God and deriving pleasure from the splendor of His presence; for this is the true joy and the greatest pleasure that can be found. The place where this joy may truly be derived is the World to Come, which was expressly created to provide for it; but the path to the object of our desires is this world, as [it says] (*Avos* 4:21), 'This world is like a corridor to the World to Come.'"

You have to work. But that's how you improve (and you accept it, because you understand the goal). In the game of life, God's like your coach, and the struggles you wrestle with are the tools He uses to make you great.

Believing in good and evil as separate realities negates the concept of God's oneness.[28] Really, everything was created for the same purpose—because everything has the same source—and that source is only for good. Everything you experience in life—even if it's ugly or unpleasant—is only coming for the sake of getting you closer to God.

LOVE GOD

According to the Torah (Deuteronomy 6:5), you're supposed to "Love God with all your heart, with all your soul, and with all your possessions."[29] Specifically:

- "With all your heart" means your desires. You achieve this level when your deepest desire is to fulfill God's will.
- "With all your soul" means using all your physical abilities to serve God. That may even mean accepting pain, making sacrifices, or giving up your life (the Talmud defines "all your soul" as "even if it takes your soul").
- "With all your possessions" means using all your

---

28. *Berachos* 60B: "A person should accustom himself to say, 'Everything that God does, He does for the good (כל דעביד רחמנא לטב עביד).' "
29. "Possessions (מאדך)" is usually translated as, "with all your might." See *Berachos* 54a: "'With all your heart' means your two inclinations: your good inclination (יצר טוב) and your evil inclination (יצר הרע). 'With all your soul' means even if God takes your soul. 'And with all your might' means either a) with all your resources (or possessions), or b) with every measure God metes out to you (whether good or bad), you are to thank Him."

resources to serve God, which could mean spending money to fulfill a commandment (like buying a mezuzah, Hanukkah candles, or matzah for Passover), losing money rather than transgressing a mitzvah, or giving charity.

Love is defined as "identifying virtue in another person, and identifying those virtues with that person."[30] Everything about God is virtuous, and the most direct way to love Him is to see—or come to appreciate—those virtues in action. Part of how you do that is by studying three things: nature, history, and Torah:

- Nature, and by extension, science, teaches you the genius, beauty, symmetry, balance, and perfection of God's world. The better you understand that, the more you come to appreciate that the world you live in is an incredible gift.
- History is both personal and national. Knowing your personal history—your story—is how you see God's hand in your life. Jewish history teaches you about providence, and the miracle of Jewish survival.
- Torah is the message God gave the Jewish people. As you plumb its depths, you come to love and appreciate God's infinite wisdom.

You are wired to love God, which explains why man—as long as he's alive—can never be satisfied or at peace. Your true inner yearning is for God, which is Infinite. That's endless. It can never be satiated by anything finite or physical. A person

---

30. The source for this definition of love is from the book of Leviticus, 19:18: "Do not take revenge nor bear a grudge against the children of your people. You must love your neighbor as [you love] yourself. I am God." When you take revenge or bear a grudge, you're harboring resentment, or focusing on the negative. Love is the opposite, which comes from focusing on, and appreciating, the positive.

is designed to appreciate the infinite. Anything less leaves you empty and lacking.

Fear God

Fear, or *yirah* (יראה), also means "to see." In other words, "fearing God" means seeing, or recognizing, the consequences of your actions. Life is serious business, and you need to understand that there are consequences—both rewards and punishments—for every moment you're alive.

You can acquire that with daily reflection and introspection, which includes working through these five steps:[31]

One: This world is overflowing with pleasure

No matter how you look at it—whether it's physical pleasures, love, meaning, creativity, or even transcendence—the opportunities for pleasure are endless. Appreciate how much you're missing, and how different your life would be if you lived every moment to the fullest.

Two: You would give up those pleasures to avoid the pain of this world

The pleasure of this world doesn't compare to the pain. Consider, God forbid, the pain of losing a child, witnessing the evils of the Holocaust, or the ravages of war and disease. The heartbreak is unimaginable, and far outweighs the pleasure available. When you're aware of that pain, your reaction is, "How can I avoid it?"

Three: One moment in hell is more painful than all the pain of this world

The first two levels are what the body experiences, which is temporary. But the next world is about the soul, which is

---

31. *Avos* 4:22: "Better one hour of repentance and good deeds in this world than the entire life of the world to come; and better one hour of spiritual bliss in the world to come than the entire life of this world."

eternal. The shame and regret that the soul feels from one mistake is far worse than the combined total of all the pain of this world. Imagine what that must be for truly terrible people.

Four: The experience of hell is nothing compared to the reward of doing one mitzvah

Hell is the soul's shame, but a mitzvah is an eternal connection to God. The opportunities to perform mitzvahs are seemingly endless, and even include actions as simple as saying "good morning," or a sincere moment of prayer.

Five: The reward for mitzvahs is nothing compared to doing God's will

When you understand reality, you recognize that concepts like reward and punishment are inferior motivators. They betray a lack of comprehension about the value of doing God's will. God is the only reality, and living with that reality is the only point of existence.

A God-fearing person is real. You understand that God's existence is the only existence, and live your life with the clarity of that conviction.[32]

---

32. *Shabbos* 31:A: "When a person is brought to his final judgment, he's asked, 'Were you honest in business? Did you set time to study Torah? Did you try to have children? Did you wait for the Messiah? Did you delve into wisdom? Did you infer deeper ideas, one from the other?' But even so [meaning: all this is of little consequence], if fear of God was his 'storehouse,' then yes [his judgment is favorable], and if not, no." See there for more examples. Also see *Yoma* 72:B: "Rava said to his rabbinical students, 'I beg you, don't earn Gehinnom twice.'" According to Rashi, that means, "Don't study the Torah without fulfilling it [i.e. without fear of God]. If you do, you experience Gehinnom in this world because you deprived yourself of worldly pleasures, and also the next world for failing to fulfill the Torah."

DON'T STRAY AFTER YOUR HEART AND EYES

"Heart" refers to your desires, and "eyes" refers to distractions, and, similar to not believing in other powers, these are constant temptations.

Your heart—or desires—has two levels: the desires of your soul (called your "good inclination" or yetzer tov/יצר טוב), and the desires of your body (called your "evil inclination" or yetzer hara/יצר הרע).[33] Your soul is the voice that tells you what you *want* to do, as opposed to your body, which tells you what you *desire* to do. That dichotomy between soul and body is a constant struggle, and it takes a lifetime of effort to learn to follow after the ambitions of your soul, and to not get pulled after the temptations of your body.

Unlike your heart, which is an internal battle, your eyes are focused on the external, and that's also a constant temptation. You need to avoid impossible situations, which applies in varying degrees: from not testing yourself with challenges that are antithetical to your goals,[34] to not trying to be something you're not. Know yourself, set realistic goals, and avoid trails you're destined to fail.

The goal of living a Jewish life is to instill within you an awareness of the reality of God's existence (and oneness). Your body is designed to prevent that from happening. That's your challenge, and it's a lifetime of effort.

---

33. Numbers 15:39: "Don't go after your heart and eyes after which you stray." "Your heart" (לבבכם) is spelled with an extra "beis (ב)." One beis (ב) refers to your soul, and the other, your body.

34. If you're on a diet, don't buy a cake that you're "not going to eat"

Section Three: Integration

SEVEN STEPS TO HUMILITY

Humility is the ability to see reality. It has nothing to do with weakness. It's understanding that God is the only reality. God is your source, and everything comes from Him.

But being humble is difficult. Acquiring humility is a constant battle against your evil inclination (יצר הרע), which, from its—or really *your*—perspective, sees itself as the center of the universe. Learning to see things differently takes a lifetime of effort.[35]

In Jewish thought,[36] one approach to acquiring humility is meditating on these seven ideas:

One: Don't identify with your body. Identify with your soul.

Two: You're not your body. You have a body. The body doesn't define you.[37] Recognize that your soul is, so to speak, a part of God.

---

35. "Instead of viewing life from an *ego*centric perspective, man's challenge is learning to view life from a *theo*centric perspective." Heard from Rabbi Yochanan Zweig

36. *Duties of the Heart*, Gate of Humility, Chapter 5

37. *Jewish Meditation: A Practical Guide*, by Rabbi Aryeh Kaplan, pages 87–88:

> "The Kabbalists point out that the body is not the self. Since I can speak of 'my body,' the body cannot be 'me.' The body is

Three: Your soul is constantly seeking greatness. Your body is easily distracted. For example, if you're feeling miserable or tired, that's a message from your body. Don't identify with that voice. Identify with your soul, which wants to be great.

Four: Realize that whenever you choose your body over your soul, it pulls you down. For example, if you overeat

---

'mine'—something associated with me; but the ultimate me is something much more profound than the body. Using the same argument, I can also speak of 'my mind.' Indeed, I speak of 'my mind' just as I speak of 'my body.' This would imply that just as the body is not the real me, the mind is also not the real me. Carrying the argument a step further, I can even speak of 'my soul.' This would imply that even the soul is not the real me.

This being the case, the question of selfhood becomes very difficult indeed. What is the real me? A hint to the answer can be found in the Hebrew word for 'I,' *ani* (אני). It is significant to note that if the letters of *ani* are rearranged, they spell the word *ayn* or *ayin* (אין), which denotes nothingness. This would seem to imply that the real 'me' is the nothingness within me.

This can be understood in a fairly straightforward manner. The real me is my sense of volition. It is the intangible will that impels me to do whatever I decide to do.

* * *

As I noted, neither the body, the mind, nor the soul is the self. However, in another sense, the self is a combination of body, mind, and soul. The three together appear to define the self.

However, this has an important ramification. If body is not the self, and mind is not the self, and soul is not the self, but the combination of the three is, then the definition of the self is still an enigma. It would seem that it is possible to remove the body, remove the mind, and remove the soul, and still have some spark of the self. But when body, mind, and soul are removed, all that remains is nothingness. Again it appears that the self is nothingness.

It is not nothingness because of lack of existence. Rather it is nothingness because of the lack of a category in the mind in which to place it."

or oversleep, you feel disgusted. But when you identify with your soul, you feel fantastic.

Five: Compare your body and soul: the body is just another physical object; another one of the billions of people alive in the world. Beyond that, humanity is just one of the myriad creatures alive on earth. The earth is just a part of a much larger solar system, and the solar system is just a speck of the universe.

But your soul is a direct link to God. God encompasses and transcends the entire universe. When you're connected to God, you're connected to eternity.

Six: Recognize the difference between body and soul. The body is finite and limited. The soul is infinite. The body is limited by time, and will eventually die. The soul transcends that.

Seven: Your greatest accomplishments are when you identify with your soul, and your biggest blunders are when you identify with your finite, limited body.

Humility is when you identify with your soul to the detriment of your body or ego. You understand your source, and you live with that reality.

PRAYER

Prayer is an opportunity to refine and affirm what you want out of life. It's a way to express your desires, and is an extension of your free will. In Jewish thought, God is considered infinite, all-knowing, and all-powerful. He knows your wants and needs, and more than that, He has the ability to deliver. Prayer, obviously, isn't for God.

Prayer is for you.

God answers every prayer, but that doesn't mean you always get what you want. Sometimes the answer is "no." If God gave you everything, your life would be easy and comfortable, but you would also remain shallow and undeveloped. You would not grow as a person, or fulfill your spiritual potential. The challenges you face, and the work that you do, is how you learn to appreciate and value your life. Prayer gives you an active role in that process. It initiates a conversation with God, and forces you to ask, "What is God trying to tell me?"

The Jewish approach to prayer starts with the premise that God *already knows* what you want. However, you need to review. These five steps are a practical approach to getting the most out of Jewish prayer.

One: Define your terms. Are you clear about what you are praying for? Are you sure it is in your best interest?

Two: Make an effort. Prayer isn't an escape from effort and responsibility. It isn't magic. What are you willing to do to make your prayer a reality?

Three: Expect the good. If you don't expect that God will answer your prayer, He won't surprise you with success. He wants you to come to the realization that you can always count on Him.

Four: Be shocked if the answer is no. Nothing God does is an accident. If things do not go smoothly, your first reaction should be one of surprise. "Why is God doing this? What is He trying to tell me?" God wants a relationship, but sometimes He needs to get your attention.

Five: Listen to what God is telling you. God is always teaching and guiding you, but sometimes the most important lessons are difficult to accept.

The Torah mentions the idea of daily prayer in Exodus 23:25, "You shall *serve* God,"[38] and again in Deuteronomy 11:13,

---

38. According to the Talmud, *Baba Metzia* 107B, the worship referred to in Exodus 23:25 is both the daily recitation of the Shema and prayer.

"And you will *serve* God with all your heart." According to the Talmud,[39] prayer is the "service" that's done with your heart.

But the Hebrew word, "to serve (עבודה)," also means "work." Prayer is work. It's a daily opportunity to involve God in your life, and that takes discipline, consistency, effort, and patience.

---

39. *Taanit* 2A

*"You need to know
what you're willing to die for
in order to know
what you're willing to live for."*

PART II:
RESPONSIBILITY

Section One:
Personal Responsibility
(Harnessing the Power of Free Will)

God created the world for your benefit and pleasure, and the greatest benefit—and your ultimate pleasure—is the opportunity to emulate, and, as a consequence of that, have a relationship with God.

But the onus is on you. The strength of that relationship is dependent upon how much you want it, or how much you're willing to work for it. That's your choice.

That freedom to choose—and specifically, that freedom to choose a relationship with God—is a cornerstone of Jewish belief.

In Jewish thought,[1] when the Torah says (Genesis 1:27), "God created man in His image," it's referring to man's ability to choose, also called "free will." According to the Talmud (*Avos* 3:18), "Man is beloved, because he was created in the image of God," meaning that free will is more than just a state of being, it's a gift.

Free will is unique to man. Free will is power. Free will is the ability to shape the world. If you use your free will

---

1. See the *Sforno* on Genesis 1:26–27

correctly, you will beautify and enhance the world. If not, you will destroy it.[2]

According to the book of Psalms (8:4–6), that power is almost God-like: "When I look at the heavens—the work of your fingers, the moon and the stars that you have set in place— what is man that you should remember him, and the son of man that you should care for him? Yet you have made [man] *a little less than God*, and crowned him with honor and beauty."

The gift of free will is the power to change the world— yours and the world around you—and that's your responsibility.

In Jewish thought, free will is narrowly defined. It isn't a preference, like choosing chocolate instead of vanilla ice cream (even if that technically is a choice you're making). It's also not a choice between good and evil, because most people—even terrible people—rationalize their choices to make them seem good in their eyes.

Rather, free will is a choice between life and death.

The Torah says that as well (Deuteronomy 30:19), "I have placed before you life and death, the blessing and the curse. You must choose life, so that you and your descendents will survive."

But what kind of choice is that?

Death is avoiding pain—it's an escape—or specifically, an escape from responsibility. Every moment you're alive, you're using your free will to choose between life and death, reality or escape, being responsible or running away. That's a constant

---

2. *Nefesh Hachaim* (1:3) "God gave man control over innumerable powers and worlds, and handed them over to him in [a way] that he commands and directs them according to his specific actions, speech, and thoughts together with his behavior, be that for the good or the opposite ... that is the meaning of 'God created man in His image...' Just like God is the ultimate power over all existence in every world, arranging and controlling everything each moment as per His will, so to God [empowered] man to open and close myriad powers and worlds according to the details of his behavior in everything he does, and at every moment..."

choice. You are either making the choice to take the pain in order to grow, or you're quitting.

Being alive means embracing responsibility, and how you resolve that conflict—between reality and escape—is where your greatness lies. Choosing life is choosing to live, to fight, and to accomplish; as opposed to running away.

Mystically speaking, that conflict is described as a conflict between body and soul. According to the Torah (Genesis 2:7), "God formed man from the dust of the ground, and breathed into his nostrils a breath of life." Your body is made from coarse physical matter, and your soul is a breath from God. Those two forces are in constant conflict.[3] Your job is to identify with your soul, and to avoid the distractions, and desires, of your body.

But free will is deeper than that, too, and ultimately, it's more than just asking yourself, "What does my soul want?" It's asking yourself, "What does God want?"[4] It's aligning your will with the most powerful force in existence. It's connecting with the infinite, and syncing your will to eternity.

YOU'RE WIRED FOR PLEASURE

God created you in order to give you pleasure, and you are, by design, a pleasure seeker. According to the book of Genesis, when God created the first people, he put them in the Garden of Eden (גן עדן), which literally means "the Garden of Pleasure."

---

3. *Sukkah* 52A: "Rabbi Yitzhak said: A person's [evil] inclination overpowers him each day, like it says (Genesis 6:5): 'Only evil all day.' Rabbi Shimon ben Lakish said: A person's evil inclination overpowers him each day and tries to kill him, like it says (Psalms 37:32): 'The wicked watches the righteous and tries to kill him.'"
4. *Avos* 2:4: "Do His will as though it were your will, so that He will do your will as though it were His."

The greatest pleasure is to be at one with God. It's to unite your soul with the source of goodness and pleasure, and to have such a keen awareness of God that everything you do is accompanied by a sense of His guidance and love.

But that awareness comes at a cost: gratitude. You have to learn to appreciate the good that God does for you, to give up the illusion that you alone are responsible for your achievements, and to admit that everything you have is a gift from God.

HAPPINESS IS A CHOICE

Happiness is taking pleasure in what you have. Happiness is a choice, and a state of mind. The Talmud asks (*Avos* 4:1), "Who is rich?" And answers, "The person who is happy with what he has." If you're happy with what you have, you'll feel like a rich man. If you cannot appreciate what you already have, you'll never feel satisfied no matter how much you get.

But that's on you. Focusing on what you have—as opposed to what you don't—is a choice. That takes work, and, at times, may even be difficult. Not making an effort is easier.

Except that not making an effort—and not seeing the good in your life—leaves you feeling unhappy, which is the default: when you don't appreciate what you have, you think about what you're missing. That's how humanity is wired. The body is entitled, and wants to possess everything. The effort is appreciating that you already have what you need.[5]

Some people worry, "If I know the secret of happiness, life will be boring." But that's confusing happiness with being complacent. Pleasure is energy, and happy people are energized.

---

5. Genesis 33:9: "Esau said, I have a lot." Compared to Genesis 33:11: "[Jacob said] 'I have all [I need].'" According to Rashi (on 33:11), "[Jacob said] I have all I need, but Esau spoke with arrogance and said I have a lot, much more than [I could possibly] need."

Unhappy people are unmotivated, overwhelmed, and unproductive. Happy people are eager to live.

That's why the Jewish day starts with counting your blessings. The daily liturgy starts, as soon as you wake up, with "thank you."[6] Start each day by appreciating that you're still alive.

That's followed with a list that acknowledges the basics: your body works, your soul animates your flesh, you have the opportunity to study Jewish wisdom, you're able to get out of bed, you're Jewish, and on and on. It's a daily meditation: focus on what you have, and that sets the tone for the rest of your day.

Each day is an opportunity for happiness. But being happy is a choice, and a responsibility.

FIVE LEVELS OF PLEASURE

As mentioned, pleasure is energy, and happy people are energized. But not all pleasures are the same, and—while it's important to enjoy every type of pleasure—it is also important to understand the hierarchy of pleasures. That awareness helps you prioritize, and invest more of your energies in the higher levels.

The prerequisites to experiencing pleasure are:
1. Be a connoisseur
2. Don't fall for the counterfeit
3. Focus on the pleasure, not the effort

Be a connoisseur: A connoisseur is a student of pleasure. He's a person who learns to appreciate the depth, nuance, subtlety, and specialness of whatever a given pleasure has to offer.

Don't fall for the counterfeit: A counterfeit pleasure is *not* a pleasure's opposite. It's a fake. It's something that, while you're experiencing it, seems like the pleasure—and feels like it, and may even convince you, temporarily, that it *is* that

---

6. מודה אני לפניך — it's also a reminder that God believes in you

pleasure—but ultimately it's an illusion, and leaves you feeling empty or depleted. Every level of pleasure has a corresponding counterfeit.

Focus on the pleasure, not the effort: Pleasure and pain are not opposites. Pain is the effort it takes to experience pleasure. The greater the pleasure, the greater the effort. The opposite of pain is *no pain*, or comfort.

Experiencing pleasure is a free will choice. It is a battle between the effort necessary to experience the pleasure versus the comfort of succumbing to effortless counterfeit pleasure. That dichotomy of effort versus comfort is the struggle between body and soul.

The five levels of pleasure, and their corresponding counterfeits, are:[7]

---

7. Rabbi Weinberg explained the source for the Five Levels of Pleasure in an email to Dr. Jim Beecham in January 2001.

I learned the five levels of pleasure from the *Sefer HaChinuch* [the Book of Mitzvah Education, written in the 14th century], but it is understood only through our manner of study. He writes: "It is proper that we arrange on our hearts constantly [meaning we are always aware] that all there is in this universe, from wealth to children, to honor and power—all of these are like nothing, worthless, and but confusion, compared to the love of God."

Now, the way we study and understand the writings of an author of this stature (he is of the historic period called the *Rishonim*) is that if he states "all there is in this universe" and gives a list, he means exactly that—this is all there is in the universe. I explain wealth as material possessions, children as love, honor as seeking meaning and good, and power as power.

The *Chinuch* goes on to say, "all of these are like nothing, worthless, and confusion." An author of his stature doesn't write something like "it's not worth ten cents, it's not worth ten dollars, it's not worth a million dollars"—that's silly. If it's not worth ten cents, of course it's not worth a million dollars. So if he tells us they are like nothing, that's less than worthless, which again is less than confusion, so I concluded that material

LEVEL	PLEASURE	COUNTERFEIT
Fifth	Physical Pleasure	Over Indulgence
Fourth	Love	Infatuation
Third	Meaning/Doing Good	Status
Second	Leadership/Creativity	Power/Control
First	God	Drugs/Cults

PHYSICAL PLEASURE VS OVER INDULGENCE

Physical pleasure is something you experience with one of your five senses. In Jewish thought, physical pleasure is an important part of living. God made the physical world for you to enjoy, and according to the Talmud, after you die, you will be held accountable for every fruit you had the opportunity to taste, but didn't try.[8]

But the secret to enjoying physical pleasure is being aware of its counterfeit: over indulgence. For example, a slice of pizza is delicious. But an entire pie is too much. The effort—or pain—involved in being a connoisseur of physical pleasure is moderation, or self control. For many people, it is difficult to stop when you know you've had enough, especially when the easier, or more comfortable choice is "more."

---

possessions are like nothing, love is worthless, seeking meaning, good, and power, all are confusion, and worthless compared to the love of God.

Since reading this into the *Chinuch*, I've come across many sources which say parts of all this.

8. Jerusalem Talmud, *Kiddushin* 4:12: "In the future, a person will have to give an explanation for everything he saw but didn't [taste]. Rabbi Lazar was [careful in this regard] and saved money and ate from each different type [of fruit] once a year."

LOVE VS INFATUATION

Love is the emotional pleasure you feel when you appreciate another person's virtues.[9] Love, similar to happiness, is a choice. You choose—and make the effort—to think about another person's positive attributes, or traits. Love isn't something that happens. It's something you do.

But love comes at a cost: commitment. Every person has strengths and weaknesses. Love means committing to focusing on a person's virtues as opposed to his shortcomings.

The counterfeit of love is infatuation, which is love without effort. It's being enamored with an idea. It's the feeling of love—or of falling in love—without making the effort to understand a person, and to appreciate him despite his faults.

MEANING ("DOING GOOD") VS STATUS ("LOOKING GOOD")

Having a cause, or doing something meaningful, is—when you take a closer look—the desire to be good, or to have self-worth. In its most intense form, doing the right thing may even require sacrificing your life.

That's intense.

But that's also valuable, because knowing what you're willing to die for teaches you the essence of being alive. But that's hard to do, and most people only enjoy the pleasure of doing the right thing in retrospect. The effort to be good—especially in extreme circumstances—is so intense, it overrides your ability to appreciate it at the time. Although in hindsight, you can look back and recognize what you accomplished.

---

9. Maimonides, Book of Mitzvahs, Positive Mitzvah #3: "Meditating [or thinking deeply about someone] will help you comprehend [that person], will bring you pleasure, and, ultimately, you will come to love [that person]."

The counterfeit of being good is "looking good," or status. It's evaluating your self-worth, and feeling good about yourself, based on external factors—like your possessions or titles—as opposed to undertaking the effort to do the right thing.

CREATIVITY/LEADERSHIP vs POWER

God is the creator, and when you are creative, in a sense, you're emulating God. The highest form of human creativity is taking your animal nature, and molding it into a spiritual being.

Creativity is rooted in thinking, which takes effort. It's also what distinguishes it from third class pleasure, or doing the right thing. For example, in an army, a private is necessary, and, at times, makes incredible sacrifices for the cause, even though, ultimately, he's just following orders. But a general gives the orders, which not only involves intense thinking and planning, but also responsibility. The private's life is in the general's hands, and failure—or worse—is the general's responsibility to bear.

The counterfeit of being a creative leader is power for the sake of power. As opposed to taking responsibility and using your creative abilities to advance a worthwhile cause, power is rooted in bullying and scheming to get your way—often at another's expense—and without bearing any responsibility, accountability, or blame when things go wrong.

GOD vs DRUGS/CULTS

First class pleasure is to be one with God. As noted above, it's to unite your soul with the source of goodness and pleasure, and to have such a keen awareness of God that everything you do is accompanied by a sense of His guidance and love. The other pleasures are lacking when compared to that. It's transcendent—reaching beyond the finite world and touching, so to speak, the infinite—and experiencing God.

The counterfeit of transcendence is taking drugs or joining a cult.[10] Experiencing God can only come after a lifetime—or an intense period—of effort and struggle, as opposed to the instant gratification of getting high or the promises of a charismatic leader.

The goal of Judaism is recognizing God in all five levels. Experiencing God is the highest level. Harnessing your creative powers and molding your animal nature into a spiritual being is the next level. Dedicating your soul's desire for meaning and goodness is third level. Loving God "with all your heart" is fourth level, and "with all your possessions" is fifth level.[11] Every level of pleasure is an opportunity to experience God.

Accounting

The book of Genesis, when discussing Abraham's final years, says (Genesis 24:1), "Abraham was old. He came with his days," which implies that he used every day to its fullest extent.[12] At the end of his life, he died with "*all* his days" in hand. No day was unaccounted for. No portion of his time was squandered on anything empty or pointless.

---

10. "If you ask a cult leader, 'Am I going to heaven?' He'll say, 'Yes, assuming you join the cult.' But ask a rabbi, and he won't be able to give you an answer. If heaven really exists, and it's really all it's claimed to be, it can only be something you earn after a lifetime of effort and struggle." Heard from Rabbi Yaakov Weinberg.

11. Deuteronomy 6:5: "Love God your Lord with all your heart, with all your soul, and with all your might."

12. Zohar (*Chayei Sarah* 129a) says the Torah states that "Abraham came with his days," because he used every day to its utmost potential.

Abraham was a growth-oriented person, and saw each day as an opportunity to learn, change, develop, and grow; to get a little closer to fulfilling his spiritual mission.

That's your obligation as well, to see every day—every moment you're alive—as an opportunity.

That type of growth is expected of children. A child at 10 years old is very different from a child of five. If a 10-year-old still acts like he did when he was five—he doesn't develop, his interests don't change and mature, his language and communication skills don't advance—you would be concerned. Something went wrong. That child needs help.

That holds true when a person turns 15 or 20, too. You're expected to grow. Your body is supposed to change and mature, and you're meant to develop in other ways as well. If at 20 you're still throwing the types of tantrums considered normal for a five-year-old, you're in a lot of trouble. You won't be able to navigate society, get a job, maintain a relationship, or even do simple things like ride a bus. You would need help.

Some of that growth is natural, but most of it comes from learning lessons. It's an active process that's born from experience, be that failing, succeeding, arguing, suffering setbacks, dealing with difficult people, accomplishing a goal, overcoming adversity, exceeding expectations, and the like. Even if you fail at first, or miss the point, or you're a slow learner; over time you learn how to behave. You change and adapt. You figure it out.

That's called "growing up." You're expected to grow up. You need self-awareness—though you may also need to suffer consequences like getting lectured or disciplined—but you're supposed to grow up.

At some point that stops. An adult is expected to be different from a child. But how different is a person at 30 from a person at 20? How about someone at 40 compared to someone at 30? Shouldn't those differences be as noticeable as the differences between a teenager and a child?

When you hit 30, you've lived through another decade of experiences. Some of those experiences were probably huge, like graduating from college, or getting a job, or losing one, or getting married, or having your heart broken, or mourning a loved one. Those are significant events. They're at least as significant as a child learning to ride a bike, going to school for the first time, experiencing his body change, getting into a fight, or the myriad other experiences children go through.

Yet many people, as adults, stop growing. Life's lessons become less meaningful, or less impactful. Instead of learning, developing, changing, and growing, they wade through situations, unaffected, and hope for them to be over.

But that's not the Jewish way.

The Jewish approach is to take responsibility for your growth, and that's achieved in five steps.

ONE: SET GOALS

Growth starts with setting goals, which starts with self-awareness, definitions, decisions, and commitments. When you're clear about your priorities and values, you will set realistic goals that serve as benchmarks along the way. As you work through the steps below, you'll make changes in order to stay focused and achieve your goals.

TWO: TAKE RESPONSIBILITY

Once you have a goal, decide that you are responsible to achieve it.[13]

---

13. See *Avos* 1:14: "[Hillel] used to say: 'If I am not for myself, who is for me? But if I am [only] for myself, what am I? And if not now, when?'"

THREE: CLARITY

If you get stuck, that's because you're not clear. Ask yourself:

- What is confusing me?
- What is holding me back?

In Jewish thought, clarity is considered an important tool.[14] It causes you to act. If you're not acting, you're not clear. Figure out why.

FOUR: TAKE AN ACCOUNTING

Setting goals, taking responsibility, and being clear is a daily effort that starts with taking a spiritual accounting.

Every day, ask yourself:

- What am I living for?
- What do I need to change?
- What am I going to do about it?

FIVE: STRATEGIZE

Make a plan, be flexible, and adjust as situations change.[15] The point is to stay focused and aware. Your goal is self-awareness. No day should be unaccounted for. No portion of your time should be squandered on something empty or pointless.

---

14. Rabbi Moshe Chaim Luzzatto, *The Path of the Just*, chapter one. "The foundation of piety, and the root of perfect spiritual work, is to become clear, and to recognize as true, [your] purpose in life."

15. *Berachos* 17A: "A person should always be cunning in [regards to] fear of God." According to Rashi, that means you should devise a cunning strategy to defeat your evil inclination.

Section Two:
Communal Responsibility

Every Jew harbors a secret desire to be the Messiah—you want to be the person to discover the cure for cancer, to bring humanity together, to solve the world's problems—in other words, you want to be great.

But that's just scratching the surface, really, you want to be like God Himself, which is also one of the 613 commandments, "To be like God."[16] According to the Mishna (*Sanhedrin* 4:5), "Each and every person is obligated to say, 'The world was created for me,'" in order to understand that the world is your responsibility.

SEVEN LEADERSHIP TRAITS

Communal responsibility starts with community leaders. That means accessing the leadership traits that exist within yourself. A Jewish leader embodies seven essential traits.

---

16. Deuteronomy 28:9: "And you should walk in His ways." According to the *Sifri* (Deuteronomy 11:22), "Just as God is called gracious, you should be gracious. Just as God is called compassionate, you should be compassionate, etc."

ONE: INDEPENDENCE

A leader is an independent thinker. He knows his convictions, which start with belief in God and the centrality of Torah. He reevaluates the foundations of his beliefs, and ensures they are based upon compelling evidence.

TWO: PEOPLE ARE POWERFUL

A leader recognizes that he was created in God's image. He has free will, which means he has the power, and therefore, the obligation to change the world. That power is universal—every person has that ability—and a leader understands how to access that power.

THREE: FEAR

A leader knows that pain and frustration are insignificant when compared to the infinite reward of doing God's will. He knows that God is real. He understands that God's existence is the only existence, and lives his life with the clarity of that conviction.

FOUR: TRUST

A leader knows that God a) is the only power, b) loves him, and c) wants him to succeed in doing His will.

FIVE: LISTENS

A leader understands the necessity of listening to others, and that he may be wrong. He has the discipline to hear, evaluate, and accept different perspectives; and strives to clarify each situation on its individual merits.

SIX: PATIENCE

A leader has the patience and perseverance to pursue ideas that make sense. He knows that change takes time, but is inevitable when the idea is true.

SEVEN: JOY

Joy is the pleasure you feel when anticipating good. A leader is in touch with that pleasure, uses it to fight for the most important cause, and anticipates the pleasure of the future reward he will receive.

SANCTIFYING/DESECRATING GOD'S NAME /קידוש השם) (חילול השם):

The obligation to sanctify God's name—and to not desecrate it—applies even in situations where you have to forfeit your life. According to the Talmud,[17] which gives a number of examples and qualifications, a group of Jews—any Jews, religious or secular—should not see your behavior and come to the conclusion that you're willing to abandon your Jewish beliefs in order to save your life. That rule applies even though it's unclear what impression your sacrifice will make on their outlook or beliefs.

That also means countering thought leaders, popular figures, ideological fads, or even societies—be they bad actors, their followers, or others—who denigrate the idea of belief in

---

17. See *Sanhedrin* 74B, in times when evil governments make anti-Jewish decrees, and even in times of peace, but when a nefarious evil-doer is coercing you in public—meaning in front of a group of 10 or more Jews—you're obligated to give your life. According to Rabbi Weinberg, "Ten Jews shouldn't think that you're afraid to die, or that you're willing to transgress God's will, in order to save your life. If so, that's considered a desecration of God's name." (Lakewood Seminar, beginning of part 1)

God, the validity or veracity of the Torah, or slander the Jewish people. In such situations, you have an obligation to act. If you do, you're sanctifying God's name. But if you stand still, you're doing the opposite.

According to Maimonides,[18] a different, deeper aspect of that idea is if a religious Jew steals, or if a Torah scholar doesn't pay his bills on time. That's also considered a desecration of God's name, because people will conclude that Torah observance is meaningless.

But Torah observance and study are meaningful. It aligns your will with reality. And if that's true, and it *has* impacted you, but you feel intimidated, or you're afraid to have a conversation with a person who does not share your beliefs—even if that person is intelligent or has a PhD—that's considered a desecration of God's name.

When you interact with people, they should feel the impact and power of Jewish wisdom. It should be palpable, and that sanctifies God's name.

LIGHT UNTO THE NATIONS

Jewish ideas changed the world.

In the ancient world, literacy was at about one percent—although in the more advanced civilizations of Greece and Rome it was a little bit higher—gender selection happened at birth, with baby girls, as well as babies with deformities, often left out to die; justice, when it happened, was for the elite, but not for the serfs or peasants who worked the land; war was an almost constant; conquered populations were enslaved and exploited; people were killed for sport; and the poor were despised, but also kept impoverished as a means of control.[19]

---

18. Mishna Torah, Foundations of Torah, 5:11.
19. Adapted from *World Perfect* by Ken Spiro (Simcha Press, 2002).

The ancient world didn't accept as a given modern ideals like universal education, social responsibility, basic human dignity, equality before the law, charity, peace, or a living wage, and they certainly didn't consider them unalienable rights.

It took centuries, but that changed as the world came to embrace, and to appropriate as their own—by way of the Bible, Christianity, Islam, modern democracy, the Enlightenment, and a plethora of other movements and isms—the core tenets the Jewish people professed for millennia.

The Jewish people changed the world, and did that while being persecuted, oppressed, exiled, massacred, isolated, marginalized, and despised. Jews don't preach, proselytize, missionize, or actively seek converts. Judaism isn't a religion of persuasion, and Jews aren't the world's teachers.

Jews are an example.

According to the book of Isaiah 42:6, "I, God, have called you in righteousness. I took your hand, created you, and made you a treasured people. *[To be] a light for the nations.*" The Jewish people are called "a light for the nations," although the way you illuminate the world is not obvious. According to an earlier verse in the book of Isaiah (2:3),[20] "Many peoples will go and say, 'Come let us go up to the Mount of God, to the Temple of the God of Jacob, that He may teach us His ways and we may walk in His paths.' *For the Torah will go forth from Zion and the word of God from Jerusalem.*"

As a Jew, you will be watched, judged, and held to a different standard. You will be different and expected to act differently. And that's by design—it may even be a proof of God—the world is desperate for Jewish leadership, and you're expected to lead by example.

---

20. According to the Malbim on Isaiah 42:6, the "light" in "light unto the nations" is the "Torah that goes out from Zion."

But what if the Jewish people don't know how to be that example? When they're ignorant of their heritage, and conflate foreign—or crazy, or nice-sounding—ideas with pillars of Judaism?

That's on you.

You're not obligated to teach the world, but you do need to teach your fellow Jew. When you do, you're aligning your will with the most powerful force in the universe—the only power and source of existence—your Father in heaven, who created the entire world for your benefit and pleasure.

"Clarity or death."

Aish Glossary of Terms

ACCOUNTING:

It says in the book of Genesis (24:1), "Abraham was old. He came with his days." That expression, "He came with days," teaches how serious a person Abraham was: he used every day to its fullest possible extent.[1] At the end of his life, he literally came with "all his days" in hand. No day was unaccounted for. No portion of his time was squandered on anything empty or pointless.

You need to live that way as well, and that starts with doing a daily spiritual accounting. Every day, ask yourself:

- What am I living for?
- What do I need to change?
- What am I going to do about it?

BAFUFSTIK:

Define your terms. If you're asked, "Are you a bafufstik?" You can't answer, because bafufstik is a nonsense word. You need to first define "bafufstik" before you can say whether you are one or not. Similarly, you can't say that a visit to the Western Wall wasn't "spiritual," or that you're in "love," or that you don't believe in "God," if you don't first define what you're talking about.

---

1. Zohar (*Chayei Sarah* 129a) says the Torah states that "Abraham came with his days," because he used every day to its utmost potential.

BELIEF:

A belief is a conviction based on evidence. The amount, or quality, of the evidence may not be complete or foolproof, but it's enough to make a decision. A court of law will decide against a person—which may result in him losing his life, his children, his money, his business, or going to jail—based on the evidence, even though the judge and jury will never know with the same level of certainty as the witnesses.

In Jewish thought, belief is considered the starting point.[2] You should not take a leap of faith, and need enough evidence to say that you're making an intelligent, informed decision. Your job is to then gather more evidence until, ultimately, you can say your convictions are based on knowledge.

CLARITY:

Clarity or death. If you're not moving toward a goal that means you're not clear about something or that something is puzzling you.[3] Take responsibility. Ask yourself: what's confusing me? Clarity is your greatest tool. It causes you to act. If you're not acting, you're not clear. Figure out why.

FAITH:

Faith specifically refers to "blind faith," or "*emunah tefailah* (אמונה טפלה)," which is also defined as "bad belief."[4] Blind faith is an idea that is anathema to Jewish belief, which is predicated

---

2. *The Way of God*, chapter 1: "Every Jew must *believe* and *know* that there is a first cause ..." Belief is the starting point. Knowledge is the goal. (Heard from Rav Yitzchak Berkovits)

3. *Path of the Just*, chapter 1: "The foundation of piety and the root of perfect service is for a person *to make clear* and to come to recognize as true what is his purpose in the world ..."

4. Rabbi Weinberg translated *emunah tefailah* as "bad belief," and based on what I can find, that seems to be original to him. The closest thing to a source is Job 13:4, "But you are all inventors of lies (ואולם אתם טפלי שקר)".

on rational belief, and starts with gathering evidence and asking questions.

Faith is also defined as an emotional conviction based on something you *want* to be true. It comes from desire, and is something the body craves,[5] but isn't necessarily rooted in reality.

FATHER IN HEAVEN:

God is your Father in heaven. He created the world for your benefit and pleasure. He has the ability, and desire, to give you everything you ask for. But you have to want it. "Don't ask what you can do for God. Ask what you're willing to allow God to do for you."

In prayer, God is called, "Our Father, Our King (אבינו מלכנו)," or "Our Father, the Merciful (אבינו האב הרחמן)." He created everything, as in all of existence, for you. In return, He wants you to be happy. He wants you to enjoy life.

FIVE FINGER CLARITY:

You know you have five fingers. You don't have to be convinced that you have five fingers. If someone brought evidence that you had a different number of fingers, that evidence wouldn't shake your confidence. You have to attain that level of clarity about your beliefs and values as well. The Torah commands you: "Know there is a God."[6] Don't believe that. Know it.

In Rabbi Weinberg's class, "Know What You Know," he distinguishes between *yediyah* (knowledge), *emunah* (belief), and *emunah tefailah* (bad belief, or faith).

5. See "Free Will." Free will is a choice between soul and body: what you *want* (the ambitions of the soul) and what you *desire* (the temptations of the body).

6. Deuteronomy 4:39: "Know it today and ponder it in your heart: God is the Supreme Being in heaven above and on the earth beneath, there is no other."

FREE WILL:

Free will is the freedom to choose between what you *want* to do, and what you *feel like* doing. A free will choice is a choice between the ambitions of your soul (what you want to do), and the temptations of your body (what you feel like doing).[7] For example: you *want* to get up early, but when the alarm goes off you hit snooze, because you don't *feel like* getting up.

Free will is also a choice between life and death.[8] Do you want to live (fulfill your potential, truely be alive), or die (go back to sleep)?

GOD:

God is the creator, sustainer, and supervisor. He created the world, sustains it, and oversees everything that happens throughout the totality of existence. God is all-powerful, as in, the only power, which means that everything that happens—as in every single electron that orbits the nucleus of every single atom throughout the totality of the cosmos—only does so because of God's direct, intimate, and constant involvement. Nothing exists or happens independent of God's will. God is the only reality—and the source of all of reality—and He created everything, as in all of existence, for you.

---

7. Genesis 2:7: "God formed man out of dust of the ground, and breathed into his nostrils a breath of life." Man is a combination of body (which comes from the ground) and soul (the breath of God), and free will is the constant struggle between the temptations of the body, and the ambitions of the soul.

8. Deuteronomy 30:15-19: "See! Today I have set before you [a free choice] between life and good [on one side], and death and evil [on the other] ... I call heaven and earth as witnesses. Before you I have placed life and death, the blessing and the curse. You must choose life, so that you and your descendants will survive."

HAPPINESS:

Happiness is taking pleasure in what you have. Happiness isn't a happening. Happiness is a state of mind. The Talmud asks (*Avos* 4:1), "Who is rich?" And answers, "The person who is happy with what he has." If you're happy with what you have, you'll feel like a rich man. If you can't appreciate what you already have, you'll never feel satisfied no matter how much you get.

HELL:

One moment in hell is more painful than all the pain of this world combined. This world is temporary, but the next is eternal, and the shame and regret the soul feels from just one transgression in hell is far worse than the combined pain of this world.

Yet the pain of hell is nothing when compared to the reward of doing one mitzvah, which is the pleasure of being connected to God for *eternity*.

But even that is nothing when compared to simply doing the will of the Creator. If you understand that, you recognize that being motivated by reward and punishment demonstrates you don't comprehend the value of doing God's will. In reality, the totality of the reward of the world to come—the combined total of everything that belongs to all of the righteous people who ever lived—is nothing compared to doing God's will, which is the ultimate meaning.

HUMILITY:

Humility has nothing to do with weakness. Humility is understanding that God is the source—everything you have comes from God—and that the only thing that matters is doing God's will.

IGNORANCE:

Ignorance is a disease. It is deadly, and extremely contagious. Unlike other belief systems, the Torah teaches that man is born with an inherent desire to do good, but ignorance perverts and corrupts that desire. The antidote to being ignorant is studying the Torah, the life instructions God gave to the Jewish people.[9]

INTELLECTUAL:

An intellectual is a person who uses his *mind* to lead him through life, as opposed to his *feelings*.[10] He leads with his head, not with his heart. Having intelligence does not make you an intellectual. You could be brilliant, but allow your feelings to rule your life. The intellectual uses his understanding to arrive at reality, even if he may be less intelligent.

KNOWLEDGE:

Knowledge is an intuitive perception based on an overabundance of evidence. You know China exists, and you never need to visit to know that. The evidence is too overwhelming. You need to live with that level of awareness of God as well.

LIGHT UNTO THE NATIONS:

The Jewish people taught the world the tenets of ethical monotheism, concepts like the dignity of the individual, the brotherhood of man, equality and justice, the value of education, the

---

9. *Kiddushin* 30B: "God says, 'I created the evil inclination (יצר הרע), and I created the Torah as its antidote. If you study the Torah, you won't be handed over to the evil inclination … If you encounter the disgusting one (the evil inclination) along the road, pull him into the study hall.'"

10. *Berachos* 61B: "Righteous people are ruled by their good inclination (יצר טוב), like it says, 'My heart — the evil inclination — has died within me' (Psalms 109:22). Wicked people are ruled by their evil inclination (יצר רע), like it says, 'I think in my heart, evil speaks to the wicked saying that there is no fear of God before his eyes' (Psalms 36:2)."

centrality of family, social responsibility, respect for human life, and the importance of longing and working for peace. Ideals that nowadays most westerners hold to be "self-evident."

LOVE:

Love is defined as identifying a virtue in another person, and identifying that virtue with that person. Love doesn't just happen (you don't *fall* in love), love is something you do (you *grow* in love). Specifically, you love a person—and develop a deeper love for that person—by taking the time to identify, and appreciate, his or her virtues.

The source for this definition of love is from the book of Leviticus, 19:18: "Do not take revenge nor bear a grudge against the children of your people. You must love your neighbor as [you love] yourself. I am God."[11] When you take revenge or bear a grudge, you're harboring resentment, or focusing on the negative. Love is the opposite, which comes from focusing on, and appreciating, the positive.

MESSIAH:

Every Jew harbors a secret desire to be the Messiah—you want to be the person to discover the cure for cancer, to bring humanity together, to solve the world's problems—in other words, you want to be great.

But that's just scratching the surface, really, you want to be like God Himself, which is also one of the 613 commandments, "To be like God."[12] According to the Mishna (*Sanhedrin*

---

11. This translation, from Rabbi Aryeh Kaplan's *The Living Torah*, follows the King James Version and translates לרעך as "your neighbor," though it's probably more correct to say "your fellow man."

12. Deuteronomy 28:9: "And you should walk in His ways." According to the *Sifri* (Deuteronomy 11:22), "Just as God is called gracious, you should be gracious. Just as God is called compassionate, you should be compassionate, etc."

4:5), "Each and every person is obligated to say, 'The world was created for me,'" in order to understand that the world is your responsibility.

Pain:

The opposite of pain is not pleasure. The opposite of pain is "no pain," or *comfort*. Pain is the effort you're willing to undertake in order to experience pleasure. The greater the effort, the greater the pleasure.[13]

Pleasure:

God created you in order to give you pleasure, and you are, by design, a pleasure seeker. According to the book of Genesis, when God created the first people, he put them in the Garden of Eden (גן עדן), which literally means "the Garden of Pleasure."

The greatest pleasure is to be at one with God. It's to unite your soul with the source of goodness and pleasure, and to have such a keen awareness of God that everything you do is accompanied by a sense of His guidance and love.

But that awareness comes at a cost: gratitude. You have to learn to appreciate the good that God does for you, to give up the illusion that you alone are responsible for your achievements, and to admit that everything you have is a gift from God.

Prayer:

Prayer is a tool to refine and affirm what you want out of life. If God gave you what you needed without having to ask for it, you would never be forced to confront—or think about—your goals and desires, and you would never grow.

---

13. *Avos* 5:26: "The reward is in proportion to the pain (or effort)"

RESPONSIBILITY:

Personal responsibility is the hallmark of living a Jewish life. You are responsible for your happiness, the success of your relationships, and for your relationship with God. You are also responsible for the world around you.[14] As noted above (see: Messiah), "Each and every person is obligated to say, 'The world was created for me,'"[15] which means that the world is your responsibility.

SANCTIFYING/DESECRATING GOD'S NAME (קידוש השם/ חילול השם):

Many Jews live in complete ignorance of God, Torah, and their Jewish heritage (and the world is open, and brazen, in their hatred of Jews). If you're knowledgeable, you have an obligation to act.[16] If you act—even if you won't be successful—that's a sanctification of God's name. If you don't act—or you're afraid to act—that's a desecration of God's name.

SANITY:

The battle for life is the battle for sanity. Every person is crazy (or has the potential to be), and the only time you ever transgress is when you're overcome with a spirit of insanity.[17] Stay vigilant. If you're conscious of the fact that you may be crazy, you won't become a prisoner to insanity.

---

14. *Avos* 2:5: "In a place where there are no men, be a man."

15. Mishna, *Sanhedrin* 4:5

16. You have an obligation to give your life rather than publicly transgress God's will. It follows that you also must live your life in a way that demonstrates your commitment to doing God's will.

17. *Sotah* 3A: "A person only commits a transgression when he's overcome by a spirit of insanity (רוח שטות)".

Sin:

The Western notion of sin (an immoral act considered to be a transgression against divine law) is not the Jewish notion of sin. The Hebrew word, *chet* (חטא), which is usually translated as "sin," actually means "to miss." It's as if you're aiming an arrow, but miss the target.[18] A better word for that type of miss is "mistake."

Time:

In Jewish thought, you travel through the calendar, and arrive at various stations along the way.[19] That trip repeats itself each year, but those stations—which include the Sabbath, holidays, and other significant times—are the same. Each station is an opportunity that's available only then. If you're prepared, when you arrive at a particular station you can take advantage of that particular opportunity. If not, the opportunity will pass you by. What you make of it is up to you.

For example, the Torah calls Passover, "the time of our freedom," and Sukkot, "the time of our joy." Those times are opportunities to focus on the Jewish concepts of freedom and joy. You can work on freedom and joy at other times, too, but when you pull into the station, it's in the air. It's easier—it's the season, or the right time—to work on those things. That idea is true for the other important times on the Jewish calendar as well.

Torah:

The word "Torah" means "instructions." The Torah is called "Torat Chaim (תורת חיים)," which means "Instructions for Living." Most simple appliances come with instructions, as

---

18. Judges 20:16: "Among these people were 700 of the best left-handed men. Every one of them could sling a stone at a hair and not miss (ולא יחטא)."
19. *Michtav M'Eliyahu*, volume 2, page 21, by Rabbi Eliyahu Dessler

do more complex systems and tasks. Life, which is even more complicated, comes with instructions as well, and God, mankind's creator, gave the Torah—or His instructions—to the Jewish people.

TRUTH:

Every person has the ability to recognize truth. According to the Talmud, before you were born, an angel taught you everything you needed to know about the world. You were programmed with wisdom. But moments before you emerged into the world, it touched you under your nose (leaving an impression, called the "philtrum"), and you forgot everything.[20] That story teaches that you come into the world equipped with wisdom. Your soul knows everything there is to know about life, you just need to remember. More than that, you will recognize truth when you hear it.

---

20. Adapted from *Niddah* 30b, with additional details from the *Midrash Tanchuma, Pekudei* 3.

"When you first try to do something,
people will tell you you're crazy.
When you're successful,
they'll tell you how they knew it all along.
When you're really successful,
they'll tell you how they can do it better."

Aish by the Numbers

5 Levels Of Being An Intellectual

An intellectual is a person who uses his *mind* to lead him through life, as opposed to his *feelings*. He leads with his head, and not with his heart.

1. Define your terms. Without definitions, you are confused. Definitions become even more necessary when you factor in your subjective bias.
2. Say what you mean. Check your definitions before speaking up.
3. Mean what you say. Connect what you understand to your feelings and make that your reality.
4. Live what you mean. Use your mind to guide your life.
5. Walk with God. Don't do anything without being aware that God is with you, watching you and helping you.

5 Levels Of Free Will

Free will is a choice between life and death, reality and escape, effort and comfort, and your body and soul. Choose life. Be the person you *want* to be, and don't be a slave to the person you *feel* like being.

1. Be aware. If you're awake, you're making choices.

2. Don't be a puppet. Don't make choices based on your society's priorities, or other outside influences. Do what you want. Don't even allow your past, or old decisions, to dictate your choices.
3. Realize you are in a constant state of conflict. Your body and soul are at war.
4. Identify with your soul, and not your body's desires.
5. Make your will God's will, which is the ultimate usage of your freedom to choose.

5 Levels Of Pleasure

Pleasure gives you energy, but not all pleasures are equal. Understanding the hierarchy of pleasures will help you prioritize, and spend more time enjoying higher, more meaningful pleasures.

The prerequisites for understanding pleasure are:

- Pleasure gives you energy
- Every pleasure has a counterfeit, which is something that when you're experiencing it feels and seems like the pleasure, but instead of giving you energy, leaves you empty and defeated
- The way to appreciate each pleasure is to become a connoisseur of that pleasure
- No pain, no gain: pain is not the opposite of pleasure—the opposite of pain is no pain, or comfort—rather, pain is the effort you need to expend in order to experience pleasure. The greater the pleasure, the greater the effort
- No exchange rate: the distinguishing feature between each level of pleasure is that no amount of a lower level of pleasure can buy a higher level

CLASS	PLEASURE	COUNTERFEIT
Fifth Class	Physical Pleasure	Over Indulgence
Fourth Class	Love	Infatuation
Third Class	Meaning/Doing Good	Status
Second Class	Leadership/Creativity	Power/Control
First Class	God	Drugs/Cults

5 STEPS TO GET YOUR PRAYERS ANSWERED

God doesn't need your prayers. You do. God already knows what you want. But you need to review. Prayer is a tool to refine and affirm what you want out of life.

1. Define your terms. Are you clear about what you are praying for? Are you sure it is in your best interest?
2. Make an effort. Prayer isn't an escape from effort and responsibility. It isn't magic. What are you willing to do to make your prayer a reality?
3. Expect the good. If you don't expect that God will answer your prayer, He won't shock you with success. He wants you to come to the realization that you can always count on Him.
4. Be shocked if the answer is no. Nothing God does is an accident. If things do not go smoothly, your first reaction should be one of surprise. "Why is God doing this? What is He trying to tell me?" God wants a relationship, but sometimes He needs to get your attention.
5. Listen to what God is telling you. God is always teaching and guiding you, but sometimes the most important lessons are difficult to accept.

THE ABCS OF JUDAISM (IN 5 STEPS)

Embedded deep in your consciousness is the knowledge of what life is about. You have to access it.

A. Each person was born with the ability to recognize truth.

B. People, by design, are wired for pleasure. That's what motivates you.

C. You will make mistakes. Mistakes are not sins—they don't define who you are—but sometimes you will miss the mark.

D. Ignorance is the worst mistake. Don't make it. Get educated about life.

E. God gave you the Torah, which is your instructions for living.

6 CONSTANT MITZVAHS

These six commandments are the foundation of living, and thinking, like a Jew. They're constant commandments, meaning they're the basis for how you relate to the world around you.

1. Know God exists: live with an awareness of God: feel His presence, trust Him, listen to Him, take pleasure in doing for Him, and know that He loves you

2. Don't believe in other powers: God is the only power, and if you know that He's with you, you cannot fail

3. Know God is one: God is the only reality, and everything comes from Him

4. Love God: your greatest pleasure is unity and oneness with God

5. Fear God: Fear, or *yirah* (יראה), means "to see." See the consequences of your actions. Life is serious business. Understand that there are consequences—both rewards and punishments—for every moment you're alive

6. Don't stray after your heart and mind: God is the only power, believing in anything other than that—even for an instant—is like being insane

7 STEPS TO HUMILITY[21]

1. Don't identify with your body. Identify with your soul.
2. Recognize that your soul is, so to speak, a part of God.
3. Since your soul is from God, it's constantly seeking greatness. If you're feeling miserable or tired, that's your body talking.
4. Realize that whenever you choose your body over your soul, it pulls you down. If you eat too much or oversleep, you feel disgusted. But when you identify with your soul, you feel fantastic.
5. Compare your body and soul: the body is just another physical object, another person; but your soul is a direct link to God.
6. Recognize the difference between body and soul. The body is finite and limited. The soul is infinite. The body is limited by time, and will eventually die. The soul transcends that.
7. Your greatest accomplishments are when you identify with your soul, and your biggest blunders are when you identify with your finite, limited body.

7 STEPS TO BUILD TRUST IN GOD[22]

1. Realize that God loves you. Live with that awareness.
2. Realize that God's awareness is constant. He's aware of everything that happens, and hears your requests.

---

21. *Duties of the Heart*, Gate of Humility, chapter 5
22. *Duties of the Heart*, Gate of Trust, chapter 3

3. Realize that God has all the power. He can do, literally, anything.
4. Realize that God is the *only* power. Nothing happens that God doesn't allow to happen.
5. Realize that since God is the only power, everything He does for you is a gift. Appreciate that.
6. God doesn't need anything from you. Whether or not you keep the Torah doesn't affect Him. It affects you. Realize that everything He does for you—as well as everything He's commanded in the Torah— He's given you for your benefit.
7. God knows what's good for you. Trusting in God means understanding that when He doesn't give you something, He's sending you a message. He's trying to wake you up, to reconnect you to reality.

7 Traits For Building A Community Of Leaders

A Jewish leader embodies seven essential traits.

1. Independence: a leader is an independent thinker.
2. Empowered: a leader understands that every person has the power, and therefore, the obligation to change the world.
3. Perspective: a leader knows that pain and frustration are insignificant when compared to the reward of doing the right thing.
4. Trust: a leader knows he's not alone, and that with God's help, he will be successful.
5. Listens: a leader understands the necessity of listening to others, and that he may be wrong.
6. Patience: a leader has the patience and perseverance to pursue ideas that make sense. Change takes time, but is inevitable when the idea is true.

7. Joy: a leader is in touch with the power of joy—the pleasure you feel when anticipating good—and is joyful when fighting for the most important cause.

48 Ways To Wisdom

The 48 Ways are found in the Mishna.[23] Over the years, due to scribal errors—for example, dividing two aspects of a similar idea, like fear and awe, into two separate listings—the list was expanded to 50.

1. Constant study
2. Effective listening
3. Speak it out, articulate your inner thoughts
4. An understanding heart
5. Awe
6. Fear
7. Humility
8. Joy
9. Purity
10. Serve the wise man: you need a teacher or guide
11. Work out your ideas with your friends
12. Teach in order to learn
13. Be deliberate
14. Written instructions for living
15. The Oral instructions for living
16. Apply business acumen for making life decisions
17. Harness the power of sex
18. Harness the power of pleasure
19. Minimize sleep
20. Minimize conversation
21. Minimize laughter
22. Accept frustration
23. Allow your heart to guide you

---

23. *Avos* 6:6

24. Search for wisdom
25. Accept pain
26. Know your place
27. Happiness
28. Take precautions
29. Don't take pride
30. How to be loved: give love to receive love
31. Love God
32. Love humanity
33. Love righteousness
34. Love the straight road
35. Love criticism
36. Run away from honor
37. Don't be complacent
38. Don't delight in decision making
39. Empathize
40. Make other people meritorious and judge them favorably
41. Stand on truth
42. Stand on peace: bring peace to yourself and others
43. Settle your heart with learning: be fascinated with life
44. Answer and ask questions
45. Expand what you know: listen and add another dimension
46. Learn in order to teach
47. Learn in order to do
48. Make your teachers smart
49. Organize what you know
50. Say over an idea in the name of the person who said it

"Happiness is an obligation."

Essay On Antisemitism[1]

Antisemitism is defined as hostility toward, prejudice against, or hatred of Jews.

But it's more than that.

The term antisemitism was coined in 1879 by German journalist and race theorist, Wilhelm Marr, in his pamphlet, *The Path to Victory of Germanism Over Judaism.*[2] Marr expanded on themes he raised in an earlier work, which warned that Jews— as a distinct racial group, or "Semites"—were infiltrating, and diluting, pure German culture.

The term is something of a misnomer in that "Semite," especially in modern usage, is primarily used as a linguistic grouping, and refers to others, like Arabic-, Aramaic-, and Phoenician-speakers as well. But in the racist morass of 19th century Germany, it was used *specifically in reference to Jews* as a way of stressing their racial inferiority. The term stuck, and today is used almost universally to describe hatred and bigotry against Jews.

---

1. This essay is adapted from here: https://aish.com/what-is-antisemitism/, which was adapted from the "Why the Jews?" seminar, which is also posted, in essay form, on aish.com. Some content from other Aish articles (quoted in the piece) are hyperlinked within the original essay, especially the "History Crash Course," by Ken Spiro. Go online to see more.
2. This is what it looks like in German: *Der Weg zum Siege des Germanenthums über das Judenthum*

Given the term's history, many groups—including the International Holocaust Remembrance Alliance (IHRA), the Anti Defamation League (ADL), Yad Vashem (the Holocaust Remembrance Center in Jerusalem), and others—are careful to spell the term as one word (antisemitism), and *not* with a hyphen (anti-Semitism).

According to the IHRA: "The hyphenated spelling allows for the possibility of something called 'Semitism,' which not only legitimizes a form of pseudo-scientific racial classification that was thoroughly discredited by association with Nazi ideology, but also divides the term, stripping it from its meaning of opposition and hatred toward Jews." Don't allow antisemitic propagandists to cynically distort the term, or to apply it to other groups—as in "Semites"—as a way to marginalize, or diminish, Jewish suffering.

History of Antisemitism

Antisemitism is unique in the annals of history, and its distinguishing characteristics include its universality, longevity, intensity, and irrationality.

Universality: Jew hatred is ubiquitous, and since the classical era—with the beginnings of the Jewish diaspora—Jews have been subjected to hardships in the lands where they've lived, whether that's in Europe, the Middle East, throughout North Africa, or in the new world.

Longevity: Antisemitism is millennia old, and can be found as early as the Greek Seleucid Empire (at the time of the Hanukkah story), and with the Roman decrees they issued in response to their travails governing Roman-occupied Judea; but became much more focused and intense with Rome's conversion to Christianity, the rise of Islam, and the events leading up to and surrounding the Crusades. By medieval times, vicious, government-sanctioned antisemitic decrees, expulsions, and attacks were already old news.

Intensity: Anti-Jewish discrimination and second class status, while terrible, often quickly devolves into outrageous libels, expulsions, mob violence, murder, and genocide.

Irrationality: Everything and its opposite is a "reason" for antisemitism. For example, in communist countries, Jews were hated for being "capitalists;" while in capitalist countries they were hated for being "communists." When Jews live in ghettos, they're hated because they're "clannish and keep to themselves;" but when they assimilate, they're hated because they're "trying to infiltrate and corrupt the dominant culture." When Jews live amongst the nations, they're accused of "plotting world domination;" but when they live by themselves, they're called "Zionist colonialist occupiers and oppressors." Jews are "too white" to count as an oppressed minority, but not "white enough" to mollify white supremacists. Jews are also the only people accused of "killing God." Every reason, no matter how outlandish, is someone's reason to hate Jews.

EUROPEAN ANTISEMITISM

European antisemitism, while always dormant, ramped up in levels of ferocity with the onset of the Crusades.

In the tenth century, Christian Europe was gripped with "millennium fever" and the certainty that Jesus was going to return in the year 1000 (the anticipated "Second Coming").

When that didn't happen, Christians directed their disappointment and wrath at the Jews, who:

1. Had rejected Jesus in his lifetime
2. Continued to reject him (by virtue of retaining their Jewish beliefs)

The Crusades (starting in 1095) marked the first large-scale European mob violence directed against Jews, which became the pattern until modern times. It's estimated that between 30 and 50 percent of Europe's Jews were slaughtered by Crusader mobs making their way through Europe en route to liberate the holy land (where they murdered Jerusalem's Jewish community upon arrival).

And yet, in the ensuing centuries following the Crusades, the Jewish experience in Europe somehow managed to get worse. The period is marked with blood libels, which is the specious claim that Jews a) need Christian blood to bake matzah, and b) are willing to murder to get it. Blame for the bubonic plague: the plague wiped out up to half of Europe's population, and Jews were blamed, and murdered—as in burned alive—as a result. Expulsions, meaning that on numerous occasions entire Jewish communities were uprooted from their homes and forced to move. Pogroms, or wanton anti-Jewish rioting and violence. Various massacres and inquisitions. Forced confinement, like in the world's first ghetto in Venice, or in Russia's Pale of Settlement. Race laws, anti-Jewish decrees, and, ultimately, the Holocaust.

ANTISEMITISM AND THE HOLOCAUST

In the centuries leading up to the Second World War, Germany was a nation awash in racist theory: convinced of its own superiority, yet seeing itself embroiled in an existential struggle with world Jewry.

As Wilhelm Marr, the man who coined the term "antisemitism" put it in 1879:

"We have amongst us a flexible, tenacious, intelligent foreign tribe that knows how to bring abstract reality into play in many different ways. Not individual Jews but the Jewish spirit and Jewish consciousness have overpowered the world ... With the entire force of its armies the proud Roman Empire did not achieve that which Semitism has achieved in the West and particularly in Germany."[3]

Adolf Hitler, Germany's unchallenged leader from his ascension to power in 1933 until his death in 1945, marshaled his nation's considerable forces in an effort to expand on Marr's vision.

"If only one country, for whatever reason, tolerates a Jewish family in it, that family will become the germ center for fresh sedition. If one little Jewish boy survives without any Jewish education, with no synagogue and no Hebrew school, [Judaism] is in his soul. Even if there had never been a synagogue or a Jewish school or an Old Testament, the Jewish spirit would still exist and exert its influence. It has been there from the beginning and there is no Jew, not a single one, who does not personify it."[4]

Against the backdrop of the many horrors of World War II, was Germany's national mission—under Hitler's direction—to eradicate world Jewry, which today is called the Holocaust. By the beginning of 1942, nine million Jews were under German control, and by the end of the war, they managed to murder *six million* of them, or one third of the world's Jewish population.

ANTISEMITISM AND THE ISLAMIC WORLD

Mohammed, Islam's prophet, had a complicated relationship with the Jews. The Jewish people are cursed in the Koran, yet are also afforded *dhimmi* status as a "protected people," which

---

3. This is from: *Der Weg zum Siege des Germanenthums über das Judenthum*
4. Hitler's Apocalypse by Robert Wistrich, page 122, taken from here: https://aish.com/history-crash-course-61-the-final-solution/

means they can live under Muslim rule without having to convert.

Although, in practice, the *dhimmi* label means "second class," with a code of laws designed to set Jews apart, humiliate them, and emphasize their inferiority. Jews had to pay a special tax, called *jizya*, to demonstrate their subordination; they couldn't testify against a Muslim in court; they had to yield to a Muslim in public; their homes and places of worship could not be taller than those of Muslims; and more.

Jews also suffered centuries of Islamic persecution including being forced to wear items that distinguished them as Jewish; government-decrees calling for the destruction of synagogues; arbitrary confiscations of property; forcible attempts to convert them to Islam; anti-Jewish riots; and pogroms.

Despite claims that Islamic antisemitism is a new phenomenon, and merely a reaction to Zionism, examples of Islamic anti-Jewish persecution predating the Jewish return to Israel abound, including the tragic history of the Jewish community of Yemen, the Syrian blood libel, the horrors of Islamic Spain, and many others.

As Jews began returning to Israel in the late 19th century, and especially after the rise of Haj Amin Al Husseini, the Grand Mufti of Jerusalem, anti-Jewish attacks intensified—including the 1929 Hebron massacre and the Arab Revolt of the late 1930s—and culminating with the expulsion of just under one million Jews from Arab lands with the founding of the state of Israel in 1948.

ANTISEMITISM IN THE UNITED STATES

Compared to the tragic history of the Jewish communities of Europe and the Islamic world, Jews in the United States have generally been treated well. Although they did experience discrimination, especially in the decades leading up to the 1960s.

Quotas were instituted to limit their access to Ivy League universities, white collar businesses and firms wouldn't hire them, and they were barred from country clubs and other upscale establishments and neighborhoods.

Possibly the most infamous example of American antisemitism happened in late 1862, when, in the midst of the Civil War, Jews were expelled from an area called the "Department of the Tennessee," which included parts of Tennessee, Mississippi, and Kentucky.

Although American antisemitism is on the rise again.

Unfortunately, the October 7 Hamas attacks in Israel also exposed the antisemitic rot on America's elite campuses. Due to the Ivy League's outrageous response to Hamas's brutality—both from student groups, as well as college presidents and administrators—major Jewish donors started pulling their funds. As the leaders of the Leslie and Abigail Wexner Foundation wrote in a letter to the Harvard board of overseers: "We are stunned and sickened by the dismal failure of Harvard's leadership to take a clear and unequivocal stand against the barbaric murders of innocent Israeli civilians."

American antisemitism is also shaped like a horseshoe, with Jew-hatred being the one thing America's far right and far left can agree on. As noted, Jews are "too white" to count as an oppressed minority, but not "white enough" to mollify white supremacists.

According to the FBI, Jews make up 2.4% of the U.S. population, but are the targets of about 60 percent of the hate crimes linked to religion.[5]

---

5. https://apnews.com/article/fbi-hamas-attack-isis-bb1ceb7
    ce51cfc05ed751d2ce7983fcd

MODERN ANTISEMITISM

In the West, in the immediate aftermath of the Holocaust—as its horrors were first becoming known—antisemitism seemed to be somewhat diminished, although with the passage of time, it's back with a vengeance, reimagining many of the same centuries-old libels and tropes with new story lines and more sinister villains.

New trends in antisemitism include:
- Great Replacement Theory
- The Jewish people are fake Jews
- "I am anti-Zionist, not antisemitic"

GREAT REPLACEMENT THEORY

Inspired by the early 20th century publication, *The Protocols of the Elders of Zion*—the fake minutes of a meeting of Jewish elders—modern conspiracy theories claim Jews are an international, yet nationless cabal that controls international banking, the media, *and even the weather*. The American far right is convinced that Jewish interests, and particularly the Rothschild family, control the world's banks and are responsible for forest fires and other natural disasters; they also embrace extremist theories, like the Great Replacement Theory, which purports that Jews are plotting to replace white workers with immigrants, Muslims, and others.

FAKE JEWS

Another emerging antisemitic theme is promoted by groups like the Black Hebrew Israelites, who claim to be the "real Jews," and that today's Jewish community is "fake." Others make the false claim that today's Ashkenazi Jews (Jews of European descent) are in reality Khazari converts to Judaism, and, in effect, imposters.

ANTI-ZIONISM

On the left, antisemitism lives under the guise of anti-Zionism, an Orwellian theory where Palestinians are the new "Jews," and Jews are the "Nazis."

Anti-Zionists claim their positions are merely critical of Israeli government policies, but in reality they demonize Jews—regardless of where those Jews live or what they believe—and fall back on age old tropes, libels, and accusations; condone vandalism and violence; rationalize terrorist attacks; and pressure businesses, universities, entertainers, and governments to support a Boycott, Divestment, and Sanctions (BDS) campaign against Israel.

WHY DOES ANTISEMITISM EXIST?

Antisemitism is millenia old, and many thoughtful people have tried to explain it. The most common reasons given include the claims that:

- Jews are rich, powerful, and disproportionately influential given their numbers
- Jews claim to be the Chosen People
- Jews killed Jesus
- Jews are outsiders and different from everyone else
- Jews are an inferior race
- Jews are easy scapegoats

While some of these reasons may describe a particular antisemite's motivation in a given situation, none of them explain the phenomenon, especially since antisemitism happens at times and in places where these reasons aren't applicable. For example, Jews living in Russia's Pale of Settlement were penniless and weak, yet still despised; the Jews of 19th century Germany renounced their status as a "chosen people," but Jew hatred still persisted; Christians may hate Jews for rejecting Jesus, but that doesn't explain why non-Christians hate Jews; Jews are hated even when they assimilate, and do their best to shed their Jewish identity; it's difficult to call Jews a race when Jews come in all colors and sizes; and scapegoating isn't a reason for antisemitism, because you only scapegoat people you *already* dislike.

Antisemitism is the constant, while the explanation continuously changes, and given that level of malleability, the reasons seem more like excuses. Ultimately, Jews are not hated for who they are, but what they represent.

Long before any practical manifestation of antisemitism made its appearance in the world, the Torah made it known that antisemitism would play an integral role in Jewish history.

According to the Talmud, Jew-hatred starts at Mount Sinai, which—as chronicled in the book of Exodus—marks the birth of the Jewish people (Exodus 19-20). The secret is in the name, "Sinai," which can also be read, "*sinah*," the Hebrew word for hatred.

In other words, there's something intrinsic to being Jewish that makes antisemites apoplectic with rage. As Adolf Hitler put it (and as quoted earlier): "Even if there had never been a synagogue or a Jewish school or an Old Testament, the Jewish spirit would still exist and exert its influence. It has been there from the beginning and there is no Jew—not a single one— who does not personify it."

That hate stems from the dawn of the Jewish people, and—whether a Jew is in touch with it or not—somehow represents it.

THE JEW REPRESENTS MORALITY AND RESPONSIBILITY

At Mount Sinai, the Jewish people received the Ten Commandments. The Ten Commandments articulate the pillars of Jewish belief, and, according to many, are the first true expression of the tenets of ethical monotheism, or the idea that a) God exists and b) is the source of morality.

God created the world for you—your existence isn't random, or an accident—and that implies that life is meaningful. But that also implies that you are responsible. You're responsible for your happiness, and you're also responsible for your behavior. Antisemitism is a rebellion against that.

This quote, attributed to Hitler—which is eerie in its specificity—says the same thing:

> It is against their own insoluble problem of being human that the dull and base in humanity are in revolt in anti-Semitism. Nevertheless Judaism, together with Hellenism and Christianity, is an inalienable component of our Christian Western Civilization. [It is] the eternal "call to Sinai," against which humanity again and again rebels.

That "inalienable component of Western Civilization" originates at Sinai, which, according to the Torah, is when the Jewish people received the Ten Commandments and became representative of a morality many aspire to, but find difficult to attain.

Or as Sigmund Freud put it: "Jews are hated not so much because they killed Jesus, but because they produced him."

CHRISTIAN AND ISLAMIC ANTISEMITISM

That "inalienable component of Western Civilization"—the revelation at Mount Sinai—also explains Christian and Islamic antisemitism.

Christianity and Islam are belief systems derived from Judaism. They embrace the notion of ethical monotheism, the Jewish understanding of an omnipotent and all-powerful God (albeit with some qualifications), a belief in God as the source of morality, the implication that life has inherent meaning, and even the idea of a chosen people.

Except that they—Christians and Muslims—are the true chosen people.

These religions appropriate Jewish beliefs as their own, with themselves as the stand-ins as God's chosen people, or, better, as the *real* Jews. In their telling, God revised His plan, and cut a new covent with them. The Jew, without saying anything—by just existing—repudiates that belief. Christians don't hate Jews for killing Jesus, but for rejecting him. The Koran curses the Jews for the same reason: they rejected Mohammed. Jewish survival is a constant reminder that, maybe, God hasn't given up on His original covenant.

DON'T ASK, WHY THE JEWS? ASK, WHY BE JEWISH?

The irony of Jewish history is that although the Jewish people have always been a tiny percentage of the world's population (currently 0.2%), Jews are always seen as a major power in the eyes of mankind.

The reason is the message they carry: the Torah.

The world is enamored with Jewish ideas, but can only absorb that message if the messengers—the Jewish people—live them. In other words, the onus is on you: What does it mean to be Jewish? What does being Jewish mean to you?

How are you a part of the Jewish story?

"Love is a commandment."

Five Rules
of Jewish Activism
from the Alter of Novardok[6]

#1. Empower others
> Make your message easy to give over[7]

#2. Repeat yourself, often
> Your audience is distracted, make your point again (and again)[8]

#3. Take it to the streets

---

6. Adapted from *To Turn The Many To Righteousness*, from the Alter of Novardok, published by Feldheim Publishers and translated by Shraga Silverstein

7. From *Bava Metzia* 85B: A great Jewish sage, Rebbe Chanina, once claimed that if Jewish wisdom were to disappear, he'd bring it back with his towering intellect. His colleague, Rebbe Chiya, countered that the smarter way would be to gather 11 students, teach each one a different subject, and then leave them to teach each other. Jewish activism is not just rooted in the power of the message, but in empowering others to communicate the message.

8. *Eruvin* 54B: Rav Preida taught a certain student each lesson 400 times. One time, the student was distracted, and Rav Preida taught him the lesson again, which totalled 800 repetitions.

Have real conversations with real people face-to-face and in person[9]

#4. Work with influential people and leaders
They're more connected than you are, inspire them with your message[10]

#5. Remember that God already gave you everything you need to be successful, but you have to be willing to do the work[11]
"Because Moses said, 'How will I bear this alone? (איכה אשא לבדי),' the Jewish people were punished and said, 'Woe, she sits alone (איכא ישבה בדד).'"

---

9. *Yalkut Shmuel I*: Elkanah took a circuitous route to Shilo—the location of the Ark of the Covenant in his day—passing through villages and towns, and slept in the streets in order to encourage people to make a pilgrimage to Shilo during the festivals.

10. See *Tanna D'vei Eliyahu*, chapter 11: The reason 70,000 men were killed in Givat Benjamin is because the great Sanhedrin—the leaders of the Jewish nation—didn't go out and teach the people in their cities and towns on a regular basis, rather, they stayed at home and took it easy. In other words, leaders and people of influence need to support and be interested in your cause.

11. See *To Turn The Many To Righteousness*, chapter 11

*"Don't ask what you can do for God.
Ask what you're willing to allow God
to do for you."*

Aish's Vision

By Rabbi Elliot Mathias,
COO Aish Global

The vision and mission of Aish since its founding in 1974 by Rabbi Noah Weinberg has been to connect Jews around the world to Jewish ideas and wisdom. Aish has been a leader in finding innovative ways to deliver millennia-old Jewish wisdom, making it relevant to the modern Jew.

Aiming to counter the threats of assimilation, Aish has identified the root of this problem as a lack of Jewish knowledge as to what Judaism is and believes, and a lack of appreciation of how Judaism can improve both your personal life, as well as the state of the world.

Our goal is to create a transformation in the Jewish people's definition of what it means to be a Jew. We believe being Jewish means a) incorporating regular study of Jewish wisdom into your life, b) incorporating the Torah's lessons into your life, and c) sharing the relevancy of Torah with others. We believe we can achieve this definition by influencing a critical mass of Jews to embrace these three elements of Jewish identity.

How do we do this?

Thirty years ago, when Rabbi Weinberg told his students that we have a responsibility to give every Jew the opportunity to engage with authentic Jewish wisdom, we didn't understand. How could we reach *every Jew*?

But today, we have the ability to do just this. Digital media, social media, and smartphones have given us the tools to deliver Judaism to every Jew, no matter where they are. The profound and world changing ideas of Judaism don't change, but the methods and mediums at our disposal are ever-changing based on technology and innovation.

At Aish, we have jumped fully into these new opportunities and the results are startling. As of this writing, our website aish.com has over one million visitors a month; our videos on social media are being watched over 25 million times a month; and over three million people have signed up to follow us online, opting in to receive more Jewish content on a regular basis.

While these numbers are staggering, we know there is more to do. We're constantly strategizing ways to make Jewish learning more relevant, more interactive, and more penetrating to the hearts, minds, and souls of every Jew.

While technology and media are key, the soul is still the Jewish wisdom we deliver. That has been Aish's secret sauce from the beginning, and this book is a great tool to define and understand the Jewish ideas we have found best to reach and educate Jews, no matter how limited their educational background might be.

Made in the USA
Middletown, DE
13 September 2024

60399992R00068